CAMBRIDGE LIBRARY COLLECTION

Books of enduring scholarly value

Travel and Exploration

The history of travel writing dates back to the Bible, Caesar, the Vikings and the Crusaders, and its many themes include war, trade, science and recreation. Explorers from Columbus to Cook charted lands not previously visited by Western travellers, and were followed by merchants, missionaries, and colonists, who wrote accounts of their experiences. The development of steam power in the nineteenth century provided opportunities for increasing numbers of 'ordinary' people to travel further, more economically, and more safely, and resulted in great enthusiasm for travel writing among the reading public. Works included in this series range from first-hand descriptions of previously unrecorded places, to literary accounts of the strange habits of foreigners, to examples of the burgeoning numbers of guidebooks produced to satisfy the needs of a new kind of traveller - the tourist.

Journal of a Voyage of Discovery to the Arctic Regions

This journal, published in 1819 and generally attributed to Alexander Fisher, assistant surgeon of the *Alexander*, describes Sir John Ross' abortive expedition to search for the North-West Passage. Ross' own report of the voyage (also reissued in this series) was highly controversial, and William Edward Parry (1790–1855), who had commanded the *Alexander*, was sent by the Admiralty early in 1819 to continue the mission instead of his former superior. Fisher's account, which he insists is 'strictly true', begins with details of the generous provisions and special cold-weather equipment on the ships (including a form of central heating, and wolf-skin blankets issued gratis to all personnel). He vividly describes Baffin Bay, icebergs, and 'dismal' black cliffs, identified by regular compass bearings. Later, the author expresses surprise at Ross' ship turning around and leaving Lancaster Sound, although no land was visible ahead; this incriminating detail may explain Fisher's preference for anonymity.

Cambridge University Press has long been a pioneer in the reissuing of out-of-print titles from its own backlist, producing digital reprints of books that are still sought after by scholars and students but could not be reprinted economically using traditional technology. The Cambridge Library Collection extends this activity to a wider range of books which are still of importance to researchers and professionals, either for the source material they contain, or as landmarks in the history of their academic discipline.

Drawing from the world-renowned collections in the Cambridge University Library, and guided by the advice of experts in each subject area, Cambridge University Press is using state-of-the-art scanning machines in its own Printing House to capture the content of each book selected for inclusion. The files are processed to give a consistently clear, crisp image, and the books finished to the high quality standard for which the Press is recognised around the world. The latest print-on-demand technology ensures that the books will remain available indefinitely, and that orders for single or multiple copies can quickly be supplied.

The Cambridge Library Collection brings back to life books of enduring scholarly value (including out-of-copyright works originally issued by other publishers) across a wide range of disciplines in the humanities and social sciences and in science and technology.

Journal of a Voyage of Discovery to the Arctic Regions

ALEXANDER FISHER

CAMBRIDGE UNIVERSITY PRESS

Cambridge, New York, Melbourne, Madrid, Cape Town,
Singapore, São Paolo, Delhi, Tokyo, Mexico City

Published in the United States of America by Cambridge University Press, New York

www.cambridge.org
Information on this title: www.cambridge.org/9781108042246

© in this compilation Cambridge University Press 2012

This edition first published 1819
This digitally printed version 2012

ISBN 978-1-108-04224-6 Paperback

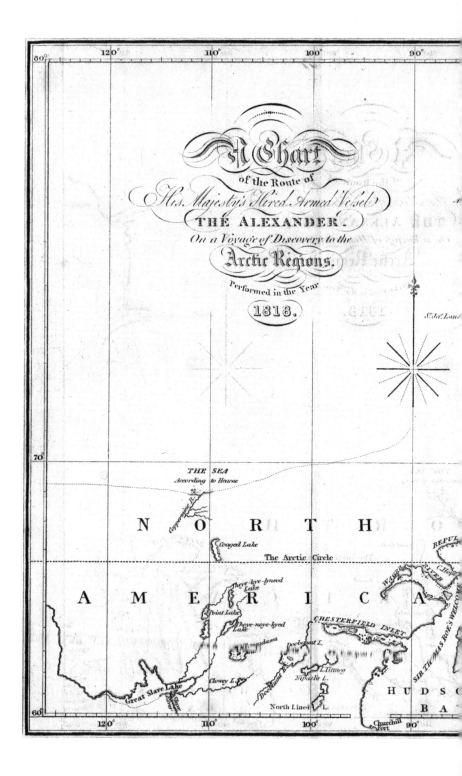

A Chart
of the Route of
His Majesty's Hired Armed Vessel
THE ALEXANDER.
On a Voyage of Discovery to the
Arctic Regions.
Performed in the Year
1818.

St Ja. Land

THE SEA
According to Hearne

Coppermine R.

N O R T H

Coged Lake

The Arctic Circle

REPUL

C. Hope

A M E R I C A

Theye-leye-lyneed Lake

Point Lake

Theye-noye-kyed Lake

CHESTERFIELD INLET

WAG

SIR THOMAS ROE'S WELCOME

saadawa

Doobaunt L.

Clowey L.

Doobaunt Lake

L.Titmeg

Nipadle L.

Great Slave Lake

North Lined L.

H U D S O

B A

Churchill Fort

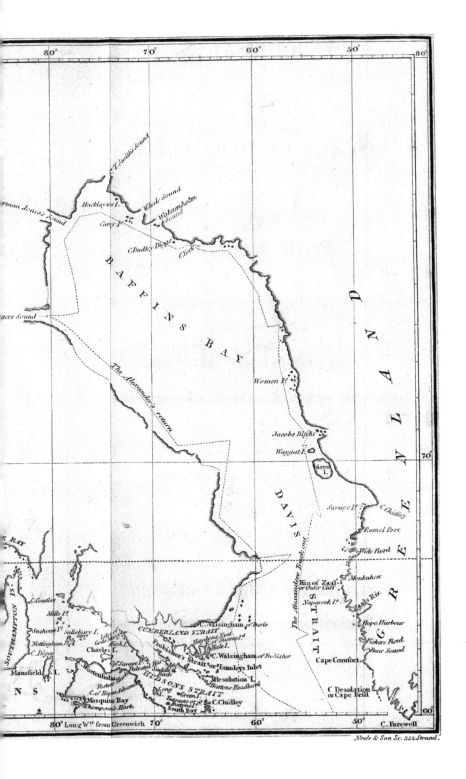

80° 70° 60° 50° 80°

rnan Jones's Sound

Hackluyts I. *Whale Sound*

Carey I. *Wolstenholm Sound*

C.Dudley Digges *C.York*

L.Smiths Sound

B A F F I N S B A Y

ic's Sound

The Alexanders return

Women I.

Jacobs Bight

Waygat I.

Disco I.

D A V I S

Savage I. *C.Chidley*

Romel Forc

Wide Fiord

C.Monkahox

Rin of Zeal or Outer Cliff *Napavick I.* *Isaks Riv.*

The Alexanders Track out

Hope Harbour

Fishers Fiord

Bear Sound

Cape Comfort

S T R A I T

B A Y

C.Comfort

Mills I.

Seahorse I. *Salisbury I.* *Isles of God's Mercy*

Nottingham I. *Rich.I.*

C.Digges *Charles I.*

CUMBERLAND STRAIT

C.Walsingham of Davis

Haydens West or Sussex I.

Hale I.

C.Walsingham of Frobisher

Mansfield I.

Wostenholm

Ft.Savage I. *Pelested Har.* *Saddle Back*

Frobisher's Strait or Lumleys Inlet

Resolution I.

Hattons Headland

Fosters Har.

C.of Hopes Advance

HUDSONS STRAIT

Mosquito Bay *Long Green*

Thompson's Harb. *Targeets or Buttons I.* *C.Chidley*

South Bay

Cape Comfort

C.Desolation or Cape Brill

SOUTHAMPTON IS.

N S

G R E E N L A N D

70°

60°

80° Long W.t from Greenwich 70° 60° 50° *C.Farewell*

Neele & Son Sc. 352 Strand.

JOURNAL

OF A

VOYAGE OF DISCOVERY,

TO THE

𝔄𝔯𝔠𝔱𝔦𝔠 𝔕𝔢𝔤𝔦𝔬𝔫𝔰,

PERFORMED BETWEEN THE 4TH OF APRIL AND THE 18TH OF
NOVEMBER, 1818,

IN HIS MAJESTY'S SHIP ALEXANDER,

WM. EDW. PARRY, Esq. Lieut. and Commander.

BY AN OFFICER OF THE ALEXANDER.

London:

PRINTED FOR RICHARD PHILLIPS;

BY G. SIDNEY, NORTHUMBERLAND-STREET, STRAND.

INTRODUCTORY REMARKS.

It having appeared, from the reports of some of the most intelligent masters of ships employed in the Greenland and Davis' Straits Whale Fisheries, that within these two years past, the Arctic Seas have been clearer of ice than they have been for some centuries : in consequence of this favourable change in these seas, and some other national motives, the British Government resolved to send out four vessels, for the purpose of exploring the Polar Seas, and of deciding, if possible, the long-agitated question—whether a passage exists between the Northern Atlantic and Pacific Oceans, through Behring's Straits ? Although the principal object of the expedition was to discover the passage in question, several others, which were deemed important, were intended to be accomplished by it ; such as that of finding where the magnetic pole is situated, and observing the difference in the vibrations of the pendulum in high latitudes. The latitudes and longitudes of places hitherto but imperfectly known where to be ascertained ; coasts and harbours to be surveyed ; and various other experiments and observations to be made, with a view of enlarging our geographical knowledge of the Polar regions. Any other facts which might be in any way useful to science, were to be collected ; and, in order that these objects might be properly fulfilled, each of the ships was provided with some of the best instruments that could be constructed, for the purpose of making the necessary observations. As it was expected that Natural History might also benefit by the expedition, a box, containing spirits and bottles, was supplied to each ship, from the Royal College of Surgeons, for the purpose of preserving any remarkable objects which might be met with in the course of the voyage.

In fitting out the ships, not any expense was spared to render them competent to the service on which they were to be employed; nor were any suggestions made by individuals neglected, whenever they were considered likely to contribute, in any way, to the accomplishment of the object in view. As it was supposed that merchant vessels would be better calculated for the service in question, than ships of war, on account of the former being better adapted for stowage, four vessels which had formerly been employed as transports were hired — their names and tonnage were as follow, viz. Isabella, of 368 tons; Dorothea, of 380 tons; Alexander, of 252 tons; and Trent, of 250 tons.

They were fortified in the strongest manner that wood and iron would admit, having, in the first place, the whole of their outside, from the keel to some distance above the water-line, covered with an extra lining of oak plank, three inches thick: within they had a number of additional transverse beams and other timbers put into the hold, in order to be able to withstand the lateral pressure of the ice, in the event of their being caught between two fields of it. Their bows were also covered with strong plates of iron, to prevent them from receiving any damage by striking against the floating ice.

They were likewise fitted up inside in such a manner as to make the accommodations of both officers and men as comfortable as the size of the vessels would admit. To guard as much as possible against the rigour of the climate, we were provided with standing bed-places, which, besides being much warmer than cots, or hammocks, possessed another advantage; for, in the event of its being necessary for us to take up our quarters on shore, they might be easily removed, each bed-place consisting of a separate box. The ships were likewise supplied with as much coal as could be stowed: they they were, indeed, ballasted with coals, so that the quantity taken altogether, was reckoned to be sufficient to last two years; and in order to warm them more effectually than could be done by the stoves alone, we had flues to convey hot air from the galley-fire, all round between decks. In the event of our wintering in the Arctic regions, we were provided with deals, Russian mats, and tarpaulings for housing the ships; and in case we should be obliged to take up our quarters on shore, the same materials would answer the purpose of roofing them. A suit of warm clothes was, together with a sort of blanket made of wolves' skins, likewise furnished by government to each of the men gratis, so that we were in every respect provided with the means of withstanding the severity of the weather.

The means of preserving the health of the crews were equally well attended to, for, besides the salt provisions supplied being of the best quality, and recently cured, the ships were provided with a considerable quantity of such articles as were deemed the most efficacious to prevent scurvy, a disease which often committed the most dreadful ravages among the crews of our early navigators, particularly in their voyages to cold climates.

The antiscorbutics with which we were furnished, consisted of a plentiful supply of Donkin's preserved meats and soups, sourcrout, essence of malt and hops, and several tons of potatoes and other vegetables. And, in case we should find ourselves in need of any articles of provision or clothing, &c. which the Esquimaux might be willing to dispose of, government supplied us with a considerable quantity of toys, and other articles of various descriptions, to barter for whatever we might want. These articles consisted of trowsers and jackets of coarse cloth, shirts, umbrellas, needles, thread, looking-glasses, cowrie shells, glass beads of various colours, and a variety of other articles calculated to attract the attention of people in an uncivilized state. Besides these, we were furnished with a number of coarse rifles to make presents of to the Esquimaux chiefs, or to exchange, if necessary, for whatever might be wanted for the public service.

And in order to facilitate any intercourse we might have with the Esquimaux, and obtain whatever information they might be able to give, a native of one of the Danish colonies on the west-coast of Greenland, was procured to go out with us in the capacity of an interpreter. His name was John Sacheuse;* he was brought to this country about two years ago in a ship belonging to Leith. Different reasons have been assigned for his leaving his own country. It has been said by some that he was picked up at sea in his canoe, having been blown off the coast of Greenland in a storm; but the reason he himself assigned was, a disappointment he met with in a love affair; having, by some means, quarrelled with the mother of his intended spouse, he failed in obtaining her consent to a matrimonial union with her daughter. The chagrin occasioned by this disappointment, affected him so much, that he resolved to banish himself for ever from his native land, and in the height of his rage set off to sea in his canoe, and was there picked up by the ship which conveyed him to this country. He was very superior in point of intellect to the generality of those who have been brought up in a rude state. He spoke English tolerably well, and could even read and write a little; but what he seemed most anxious to learn was drawing, of which he had acquired a pretty good notion. His excursions on the Thames, in his canoe, while we were fitting out, excited a good deal of notice, and I think very deservedly, for his dexterity in the management of it was really admirable.

Having now given a brief sketch of the different preparations made in fitting out the expedition, it re-

---

* He died since we returned to England.

mains for me only to say a few words respecting the probability we had of success before we set out; with respect to what has been done it is unnecessary to speak here, as it will be seen in the narrative. It has already been observed, that from the reports of the best informed masters of the Greenland and Davis' Straits Whalers, it appeared that the Arctic Seas had been within these two years past found to be clearer of ice than they had been known to be for some centuries;— but before I proceed any farther, it is necessary to observe, that in consequence of the main object of the four vessels being the same, I have hitherto spoken of them as forming only one expedition, (nor was there any distinction necessary indeed in describing the manner in which they were fitted out, as they were all fitted alike, in every respect,) but properly speaking they were two distinct expeditions, destined to take different routes, although with a view of accomplishing the same object.

From their being thus distinct from one another I shall confine the remainder of my remarks to a review of the reasons assigned in favour of the existence of a passage in the direction the expedition I belonged to went, that is, by the way of Davis' Straits and Baffin's Bay. Of the various reasons given for supposing a communication to exist between the Atlantic and Pacific Oceans in the above direction, it appears to me that the strongest argument in favour of it is, the circumstance of the sea having been seen by Messrs. Hearne and M'Kenzie at the mouth of the Coppermine and M'Kenzie's rivers; but from the superficial manner in which these indefatigable travellers have spoken of the sea seen by them at the mouth of these rivers, some people have been led to suppose that what they took to be sea, consisted merely of fresh lakes of water. It is a great pity indeed that they have not given a more satisfactory account of it, so as not to leave any doubt on the subject. If any doubt remained on their own

mind as to what they saw being the sea, they must
have certainly been very negligent, since they might
have so easily decided the matter by tasting the water,
as some persons afterwards remarked. I have no doubt,
however, in my own mind, but that they were perfectly
convinced that the water which they saw was the sea,
for it is not likely that men, after travelling so far, and
undergoing so many hardships, and so much fatigue
as they did, would abandon their object without being
perfectly satisfied, when the means which would enable them to do this were so easily attainable. If it be
taken for granted then that it was the sea which
was seen by Messrs. Hearne and M'Kenzie at the mouth
of the rivers Coppermine and M'Kenzie, it is evident
that two thirds at least of the north side of America
are surrounded by sea; for as the above rivers divide
that continent nearly into three equal parts, it must
necessarily follow that two of these parts are encom-
passed by water.

It is perhaps unnecessary to enter any farther into a
detail of the various other reasons which have been
advanced in favour of the existence of this passage, as
it is to be hoped that the expedition now fitting out
will decide the question. A list of the officers' names,
and number of men, employed on the two late expeditions, will be found in the Appendix No, 1.

VOYAGE OF DISCOVERY

TO THE

Arctic Regions,

BETWEEN THE 4TH OF APRIL AND THE 18TH OF NOVEMBER, 1818.

OUR voyage may be said to have commenced on the 4th of April, 1818, for on that day, between the hours of nine and ten in the forenoon, we cast off from His Majesty's hulk Dédaigneuse, and, in company with the rest of our squadron, namely, the Isabella, Dorothea, and Trent, dropped down to the mouth of the City Canal, which we entered about one o'clock in the afternoon, amid the hearty acclamations of the populace who lined the shore.

The Isabella and Dorothea, being the headmost ships, got through into the river; but the Trent and our ship were obliged to lie in the canal until the next day, the tide having ebbed so much before we reached the farther or lower end of the canal, that it became necessary to shut the gates. During the short time we lay here, we were, as usual, visited by several parties of ladies and gentlemen, who all appeared to be as much interested in the success of our undertaking, as we could possibly be ourselves; but, *by way of comfort,* they frequently expressed their concern for our safety in such a hazardous enterprise.

On the following day, about one o'clock in the afternoon, we got out of the canal, and, for the first time, spread our canvass to a gentle breeze, which carried us down to Galleons-Reach, where we anchored between three and four o'clock in the afternoon. Here we lay for several days, during which we took on board our powder, small arms, and various other stores of different descriptions. Among other articles, we were supplied with forty blankets, made of wolves' skins, for the use of the officers and the ship's company.

On the morning of Tuesday, the 14th of April, between the

hours of five and six, we weighed, and, in company with the Isabella, worked down to Northfleet, where we again anchored about noon. The Dorothea and Trent did not leave Galleons this morning, owing, as was understood, to the want of pilots. On the following morning, our ships again got under weigh, and worked down to Sea-reach, where we were obliged to anchor as soon as the flood tide began to make.

On Thursday the 16th, between nine and ten in the morning, we again got under weigh; and, notwithstanding the wind was against us, succeeded in working down to the Nore, where we anchored about four o'clock in the afternoon. The Dorothea and Trent were still in the river, but were shortly expected down, they having been detained, at the time we parted company, solely by the want of pilots. It will be unnecessary, however, to speak of them in the sequel, as a part of our squadron; for, although their ultimate object was the same as ours, still, from the route they were about to take, and their being under a different commander, they are to be considered as quite distinct from us.

On the morning of the 19th, we were obliged to enter Sheerness harbour, to have our windlass repaired, in consequence of some damage it had sustained on the preceding day. In the afternoon of that day, an unfortunate accident occurred, which, as it was in some measure connected with our expedition, I here insert. Mr. Stroude, superintending master afloat at Sheerness yard, having gone out to ascertain at what time we should be ready to come into the harbour, on his return, the boat in which he went out was upset, owing to some mismanagement of the crew in paying her head round. The men saved themselves by clinging to the boat, until one of our boats picked them up; but Mr. Stroude was at the time wrapped up in a great coat and a boat cloak, which incumbered him so much, that he could not lay hold of any thing, and was unfortunately drowned. His body was found a few minutes after the men were picked up, and taken on board the Isabella, where every means were tried to restore life, but unsuccessfully.

On Monday, the 20th, between twelve and one o'clock in the afternoon, we got under weigh, and ran out to the Little Nore, where we again anchored. In the course of the afternoon the ships' companies were paid their three months' advance, together with the pay due to them from the time of their joining the ships to the present day.

On the 21st, at five in the morning, we weighed and worked out to the Great Nore, where we anchored between seven and eight o'clock, A. M. About one in the afternoon we again weighed, and made sail in company with the Isabella; the Dorothea and Trent, which had arrived in the interim, still remaining at the Nore. In the evening we brought to in that part of the Swin called the Middle. Here we lay until half past one o'clock of the following day, the 22d, when we got under weigh, and worked down as far as the Gunfleet Beacon; but the wind being still against us, it became necessary to anchor when the ebb tide was done, and as, from the appearance of the weather, and the unsheltered situation, this could not be effected with safety at the place where we then were, we bore up, and anchored again at the one whence we had started. Here we found the Dorothea and Trent; but it appears that they did not consider themselves in security even at this spot, for on the following morning, the 23d, they got under weigh, and returned again to the mouth of the river. The Isabella and our ship held on, however, and on the ensuing day, the 24th, the weather becoming moderate, we got under weigh, but were obliged to bring to soon after for want of wind.

During this latter day we tried the specific gravity of the sea water along side, at high water, and at low water, and found it, at the former period, to be 1026·4, and at the latter, 1026·1. This difference is easily accounted for, and indeed is nothing more than what might naturally have been expected, seeing that, at low water, the water along side is much fresher than at high water, from its vicinity to the mouth of the river. Its specific gravity is consequently less, and vice versa.

As the hydrometers supplied to the Alexander was of Fahrenheit's construction, it became necessary to ascertain the weight required to adjust it in distilled water, in order to find the specific gravity of any other fluid; but as we could not conveniently procure any distilled water at the time, another method was necessarily resorted to, and was as follows:—The Isabella's hydrometer being a self-adjusting one, or of such a size as to displace a thousand grains when adjusted in distilled water, the adjustment of ours was obtained by the following proportion: as the weight of the Isabella's hydrometer and load, when adjusted in salt water, is to one thousand, or the weight it would displace when adjusted in distilled water; so is the weight of the Alexander's hydrometer, and its load, when adjusted in salt water, to the weight it would displace when adjusted in distilled water: from which sum the weight of the hydrometer being subtracted, will leave the weight required to adjust it in distilled water. The common divisor thus obtained was 1260·7, the weight of the hydrometer being grains 845·30, and the weight required to adjust it in distilled water 415·40.

On Saturday, the 25th, we weighed at about six in the morning, and made all sail. The wind having shifted round to the southward and westward, enabled us to get as far as Lowstoff lights before dark; and on the morning of the 26th we passed Yarmouth. It being Sunday, and the weather very fine, the greater part of the officers and men were enabled to attend divine service, which was performed by Lieutenant Parry. From this time nothing worthy of remark occurred until the 30th, on which day we made the land a little to the northward of Cape Sombero in Shetland, and came to anchor at noon in Lerwick harbour, commonly called Brassa sound, where we found His Majesty's ship Ister, and two or three merchant vessels.

On the right hand, the coast, on approaching this anchorage, is very bold and rugged, being bound with precipitous rocks, which in some places rise perpendicularly from the sea to a considerable height. In the same line of coast were observed one or two natural arches, through which the sea flowed so as to admit of a free passage for boats from one side of the rock to the other. One of these openings, or arches, much resembled, at a small distance, a piece of artificial workmanship. A few miles from Lerwick, an insulated rock, or small island, rises so close to the main land, that the chasm which divides it from the latter is crossed in a sort of basket running on a rope fastened on either side of this gulf, or opening.

The general appearance of Shetland is very uninviting, as it merely presents a uniform waste of naked and barren mountains, in some places sloping down gradually to the sea shore, and in others terminating in rugged precipices. The soil, which is of a dark mossy quality, is of a considerable depth in the vallies, and is there cut up in longitudinal pieces, and dried for fuel, they having neither wood nor coals, except such as is carried thither, the island not affording either of these useful articles. The productions of the Shetland isles are oats, barley, potatoes, and some garden vegetables. Their domestic animals are such as are common to the other British isles, unless that they are much smaller, particularly their horses, commonly called ponies. Their horned cattle are also of a very diminutive size, as are likewise their sheep; but the fleeces of the latter are of a very fine texture, insomuch that stockings, which may be drawn through a finger ring, are made from their wool I observed also that their fleeces possess a greater variety of colours than I had elsewhere seen; for in a flock of two or three dozen sheep, are to be found some quite black, others of a beautiful brown, and a variety of other shades between black and white.

The Shetlanders are of a middle stature, and well proportioned. The men are in general of a swarthy complexion; but the women are fair, and fresh and healthy in their appearance.

They are said to be extremely hospitable; and, certainly, if what we saw of them, during our short stay here, is to be adduced in confirmation of this report, they are strictly entitled to it from us. The higher classes are not inferior, either in politeness or accomplishments, to those who reside nearer the centre of fashion; they are generally educated in England or Scotland; so that, in their youth, they receive the benefits of a liberal education, and a taste for the refined manners of their southern neighbours, without having had time to imbibe those vices which are the usual concomitants of a civilized life. Although the ideas of the lower classes are, from their sequestered situation, necessarily confined, still they are very intelligent, shrewd, and circumspect; and the women are very modest in their deportment. Their chief employment is the knitting of stockings, &c., at which they are very expert.

This extraordinary address will not be deemed surprising, when it is considered that they begin to knit in their early infancy, and that it would appear to be their sole employment, until they arrive at extreme old age; for I have very often observed a band of them engaged in knitting, and standing against the wall of a house, in which were individuals from the age of ten to seventy, and I may venture to say upwards, the islanders living in general to a very great age. What I have just related respecting the employment of the women, refers only to those belonging to the town of Lerwick; for, in the country, their occupation is quite of a different, and of a more disagreeable nature. There they are literally employed as beasts of burden; for I have seen them carrying the manure on their back, in straw baskets, to the field, and drawing the harrow, beside digging the ground with their spades. This hard usage does not proceed, however, either from laziness, or a tyrannical disposition on the part of the men, but merely from necessity; seeing that almost every man who can pull an oar, sets out in the months of March and April to the Greenland fishery, so that the whole of the agricultural tasks is left to the old men, women, and children; and as the former and latter of these are not able to perform the more laborious duties, they consequently devolve on the women. The reason they assigned to us for not employing horses to labour their fields, &c., was, that they were not able to maintain them in the winter season. Those, however, who have any thing like a considerable spot of arable ground, use horses; if their ponies, some of which are not much larger than a good English sheep, can be said to merit that appellation.

Our stay at Shetland was too short to enable us to learn much respecting the customs and manners of the inhabitants.

The prevailing language is English; but I understand that some words of Norse, or of the Norwegian tongue, are still in use among the lower classes, which would indicate their origin, were any doubts subsisting on that subject. They dress in the English fashion; and this I mention as a point of distinction between them and the inhabitants of the northern part of Scotland, off which these islands lie.

The town of Lerwick, which is the capital* of the Shetland islands, is built on the face of a little eminence near the seaside, on the island probably called the Mainland, from its being the largest of the Shetland group. It is about a quarter of a mile in length, and about half that extent, or two furlongs, in breadth, and is very irregularly built, not any part of it deserving the name of a street, as there are scarcely three houses in the town built in a line parallel with each other. Notwithstanding this want of symmetry, some of the houses are large and well built. On an eminence, at the north-end of the town, stands a little fortress, containing good barracks, built, like the houses, of rough stone, and covered with slate. Its present garrison consists of a serjeant and four or five private artillerymen.

Considering the high latitude in which this place is situated, the mildness of the climate is deserving of remark; for the mercury of Fahrenheit's thermometer, in the shade, seldom fell below forty-six degrees, and between two and three o'clock in the afternoon, it generally stood at fifty degrees. I have, indeed, been told that, although the winters here are long, still they are not so severe as might be expected, being, from the insular situation, much milder than the winters in places in lower latitudes on the continent. The Shetland islands are about forty in number: of these thirty are' inhabited. The most considerable of them, in point of size, are Mainland, Yell, Bressa, or Brassay, and Unst. The whole population of Shetland is estimated at twenty-three thousand souls; and of that number fifteen hundred went this season to the Greenland fishery only, besides those who were employed in other fisheries along the coast. When we, therefore, take into consideration the number of children, and of old people, in a spot where instances of longevity are so common, it will readily appear that the effective strength of the population is, as has already been observed, during the summer months, employed at sea, consequently the chief part of both field and domestic work falls to the lot of the women.

---

* Scolloway is, properly speaking, the capital, agreeably to an old charter; but that town consists at present of a few houses only.

Having now given a brief account of Shetland, and of its inhabitants, as far as I have been able to observe them, I again resume my narrative of such facts as are more immediately connected with our expedition.

On Friday, May 1st, the day after our arrival at Shetland, Captain Sabine got on shore, on the island of Brassa, the portable observatory and astronomical instruments; but unfortunately the day was so cloudy, that the transit instrument could not be used. He found the dip, or declination of the needle, in Mr. Mouatt's garden, to be 74° 20′ 10″. It was at this gentleman's house that the observatory was erected. As it was intended that we should sail next day, every thing was got on board; but the wind prevented our sailing until the day following.

On this day the Dorothea and Trent came in, the latter in such a leaky state that they were obliged to haul her close in to the shore, in order to try if they could find at low-water where the leak was. This was fortunately discovered; or, at least, they found one or two places which were supposed to be capable of admitting the greater part of the water she made. As we sailed before they got her afloat again, we having left both her and the Dorothea in Brassa sound at the time of our sailing thence, we did not hear of the ultimate success of this repair; but it is to be hoped that all went on well.

On the morning of the third, at half past eight o'clock, the Isabella and Alexander got under weigh; and, as the wind was still from the southward, we were obliged to pass through what is called Yell sound, which, to strangers, particularly in thick weather, must be a dangerous passage, as it is interspersed with numerous rocks, some of which are above, and others just level with the surface of the water. We were, however, favoured with a fair wind, a clear day, and a native of the place for a pilot, so that we got safely into the open sea before four o'clock in the afternoon, and soon after took our final departure from the remotest of the British isles. Just as we cleared the rocks which surround the north-coast of the Shetland islands, the sky became overcast, with every appearance of foul weather.

On Monday, the 4th, we had a strong breeze, and a considerable roll of the sea from the south-east, which continued, with little variation, until two o'clock of the following morning, when both gradually subsided. About one o'clock in the afternoon a quart-bottle was thrown overboard, containing half a sheet of foolscap paper, on which were written the time and situation of the place where it was committed to the deep, with a request, in six different languages, to any person who might

happen to pick it up, to send it to the Secretary of the Admiralty. It was an exact copy of printed papers supplied by the
Admiralty, for the purpose of being thrown into the sea, in
order to afford data for detecting the velocity and direction of
currents. The printed forms are forbidden to be used by us
while in company with the Isabella, from a supposition, as I
conjecture, that those she throws overboard will be sufficient
so long as we are in company. In order to attract notice,
after the bottle is corked and sealed, a piece of white calico is
tied over its mouth, which makes it conspicuous at a considerable distance.

I believe it is intended to throw a bottle, with one of these
papers in it, overboard every day about one o'clock in the afternoon, at which hour we shall be able to have the latitude and
longitude of the ship at the time, the state of the weather, the
wind then prevailing, and the temperature of the air and water,
according to Fahrenheit's thermometer. Any other remarks
which may be deemed useful are also to be inserted. In order to
convey a perfect idea of the contents of the papers thus committed to the sea, an exact copy of the one thrown overboard
this day will be inserted in the Appendix, (No. 2.)

During the two following days nothing worthy of notice
occurred. The weather was quite moderate and fine, the
temperature of both air and water being nearly the same, the
thermometer in the former generally standing at fifty degrees,
and in the latter at forty-nine degrees. Several land birds
alighted on the rigging, apparently quite exhausted, for two of
them suffered themselves to be caught with the hand. They
had probably been blown off from Shetland by the strong
south-east wind we had on Monday, the 4th.

From this time until the 15th, the weather having been very
fine, we were enabled to try the different new instruments,
invented for, and supplied to the expedition. Captain Kater's
altitude instrument appeared to answer remarkably well, the
latitude having been obtained by it several times within a mile
of that given by the sextant. The only objection I have heard
against it, is the difficulty of observing by it when there is a
rough sea, that is, when the ship has much motion; but in
those seas where it is intended to be used, the water is generally smooth, so that there is reason to expect that it will be
then found to be a valuable instrument. Its object is to find
the sun's altitude, when the horizon is so obscured by clouds
or haze, that it cannot be found by the usual method.

The same ingenious gentleman's azimuth compasses have
also been tried, and from their light and delicate construction,
it is expected that they will be found useful when we get into

high latitudes, where we have reason to suppose that the common compasses will be rather slow in their movements.

All the other instruments we have are such, I believe, as have been used before, with the exception of Troughton's spinning horizon, which has also been tried; but I think that the experiments, or rather trials hitherto made with it, are not sufficient to warrant an opinion being given of its merits : all that can be said is, that it has not yet been found to answer the purpose for which it was intended. Dr. Wollaston's dip sector has also been tried several times, and the results of the observations made with it prove, that under certain circumstances it may be used with advantage; but the allowance for dip, as given in the tables of different books on navigation, is what will be generally trusted to. It is satisfactory, however, to have an instrument by which an error arising from any unusual refractive power of the atmosphere may be corrected. The meteorological instruments, namely, the barometer, thermometers, hygrometer, and hydrometer, have been constantly, or rather, at fixed periods, attended to, and the results regularly noted. The height of the marine barometer, and that of the attached thermometer, are taken four times every day, at regular intervals of six hours, that is, at six o'clock in the morning, at noon, at six in the afternoon, and at midnight.

The temperature of the air in the shade, and that of the sea water at the surface, are taken every two hours, by day and by night, and, whenever an opportunity is afforded, the temperature of the sea is taken at a considerable depth, by the self-registering thermometer.

The degree of moisture indicated by the hygrometer, and the specific gravity of the sea water, are generally taken once a day. Another diurnal observation is made when the weather admits of it, namely, that of the colour of the sky. This is done by the means of a small book having fourteen blue-colour leaves of different shades, each regularly numbered : by comparing these with the sky, the number of the leaf corresponding with it is noted as its colour at that time. Simple as this observation, or rather the instrument by which it is made, may appear, it has been dignified with as profound a name as any we have on board, it being called cyanameter.

About five o'clock this afternoon a white substance was observed floating on the surface of the water, and a boat was immediately lowered to pick it up. On its being brought on board, it was found to be a piece of whale blubber weighing about ten pounds : the oily or adipose substance was entirely washed away, or picked off the outside by birds, or had probably suffered partly from either cause ; for one of those birds which the seamen call malmuck (the fulmar or procellaria glacialis) was feasting on it at the time. On an incision being made into it, the inside was found to be perfectly fresh, and, agreeably to the opinion of Messrs. Allison and Philips, the master and mate, it could not have been in the water more than three weeks, or a month at the farthest. It was besides remarked by the latter of these gentlemen, that the whale of which it constituted a part, must have been killed, as the blubber of those that die is always of a reddish colour, from their not bleeding, while the blubber of those which are killed by the fishermen is of a whitish colour, such as was exhibited by this portion. Simple as the circumstance of its having been found here may at first sight appear, it will, on a few moments' consideration, be found to merit attention, as it tends in some measure to throw a light on the force and direction of the current which brought it hither, if brought by that means, of which there appears to be but little doubt. In the first place it may be asked what are the other probable means, besides currents, by which a piece of whale could be brought to the spot where this one was found. I know of two other means only; first, that of the whale being killed near the place, and secondly, that it had dropped from a fishing ship homeward bound; but, from all that I can learn, whales are never killed to the eastward of Cape Farewell, unless in the Greenland seas, and it is not likely that any of the whale ships should be so far homeward bound as this at such an early period of the season. We must, therefore, conclude that it was carried to this place by a current, either from Davis's Straits, or the Greenland seas. From the former, or rather from Cape Farewell, we were, at the time it was found, distant about two hundred leagues, and from the usual fishing ground in Greenland still farther, insomuch that it is most probable it came from Davis's Straits.

Ever since we sailed from Shetland a small bag net has been towing astern of the ship, for the purpose of securing any marine or other production, which might happen to be floating near the surface. We did not find any thing in it until Sunday, the 17th, when a species of Medusa, weighing three quarters of a pound, and quite gelatinous and semi-transparent, was taken out.

On Wednesday, the 20th, we picked up a piece of fir wood, about three feet in length, and nearly the same in circumference at the thickest end. It appeared to be the root of a tree which had been torn away from the shore by some violent means, for not any mark of an axe, or other edged tool, was to be seen on it. Its surface was, indeed, so much worn by friction against rocks or ice, that, had it been cut, the marks would have been nearly obliterated. It was in a good state of preservation, with the exception of a little of the outside, which was soft, and covered with slimy matter. From what quarter of the world this piece of wood came we were unable to say; but, from the situation of the place where it was picked up, namely, latitude 57° 50′ N., and longitude 36° 21′ W., we may reasonably conclude that it came from some part of the north coast of America.

This day, and for two days past, the weather has been remarkably foggy; but, with the exception of the chilly dampness which invariably accompanies foggy weather, it has in other respects been pretty mild, the temperature of both air and water having been, at an average, about 46° of Fahrenheit.

Friday, May 22. In addition to the reasons already assigned for supposing that the piece of whale blubber picked up on the 15th instant, was carried by a westerly current from Davis's Straits to the place where it was found, another circumstance, tending to confirm the above supposition, has been observed for three days past. The circumstance alluded to is, that the specific gravity of the sea water on the 20th and 21st, was considerably less than it had been found to-day. On the above days it was 1027·4; and to-day, at the same hour (6 P. M.) it is 1027·68. It is reasonable, therefore, to conclude that this difference is owing to a westerly current setting out of Davis's Straits round Cape Farewell, which, at this time of the year, must be considerably freshened by the quantity of ice dissolved in it. That this current should affect the hydrometer equally on the 20th and 21st, is no more than what might have been expected; for, during these two days, we were almost in the same parallel of latitude, being at noon, on the 20th, in latitude 37° 50′ N., and on the 21st, in 57° 52′ N. Again, our parallel of latitude this day, the 22d, being 57° 08′ N., may be considered as being beyond the southern boundary of this current, as the specific gravity of the sea water has been found to be as great as in any part of the Atlantic where we tried it. To what longitude this current, if I may venture to speak of it so decidedly, carries its freshness, we have not been able to determine with any degree of certainty, the weather having been so rough for some days before the 20th that nothing like an accurate experiment could be made. Prior to the above date, the 16th was the last day on which the specific gravity was obtained in a manner that could be depended on; and on that day it was 1027·7, we being then in latitude 56° 58′ 33″ N., and in longitude 25° 34′ 00″ W. It is obvious, therefore, that before the current reached thus far it lost its freshness from impregnation with the ocean. That   carries its freshness, however, for a considerable distance to the eastward of Cape Farewell is evident; for on the 20th we were in longitude 36° 21′ W., and yesterday in 39° 45′ W., and on both days we found the specific gravity of the water to be the same.

About this time we observed another fact equally interesting, and tending likewise to corroborate the conclusion drawn from the late difference of the specific gravity of the sea water. From the 17th to the 21st instant its temperature was invariably colder than that of the air, which is contrary to what we had generally found before. This change, I think, may also be attributed to the same cause as the difference of the specific gravity lately observed. The fresh, or ice water, being colder than the salt water, will necessarily affect the temperature of the whole body of water with which it is blended, insomuch that the water will probably be colder than the air, wherever this current prevails.

Yesterday and to-day several land birds have hovered about the ship, in so exhausted a state, that two of them suffered themselves to be taken with the hand. They are of the same species as those we caught soon after leaving Shetland, namely, the Wheatear (motacilla œnanthe.)

On Tuesday, the 26th, about five in the afternoon, we had a distant view, for the first time, of what ere long will probably be a very familiar sight to us, although this day it excited much curiosity. The object alluded to was a large iceberg, which was seen from the mast head at the above hour, bearing N. E. of us. About seven o'clock we got within nine or ten miles of it, and at this distance it presented a magnificent spectacle, appearing like an immense rock of white marble rising out of the sea. We were too far from it to be enabled to form any thing like a correct idea of its size; but this is to be less regretted, as we shall in all probability have, in the course of a short time, an opportunity of ascertaining the size of some of these immense floating masses of ice by actual measurement. This afternoon, both the thermometer and hydrometer indicated our approach to the ice, for the former fell to 37° in both air and water, and the specific gravity of the sea-water, as found by the latter, was not more than 1027·5. During the afternoon the clouds near the horizon, towards the north-west, presented an unusual white appearance, in some places resembling snowy mountains rearing their summits out of the ocean. For this day, and for several days past, the colour of the water has been observed to be considerably changed; for, instead of that clear blue colour it had all the distance from Shetland to the longitude of Cape Farewell, it has now a light brownish colour when the weather is clear, and, when foggy or hazy, a turbid appearance, such as I have generally observed at the estuary of large rivers.

The specific gravity of the sea water we find to be diminishing daily. At six o'clock in the evening of the 27th, it was only 1027·2, the temperature of the water at the time being 44°. Two days before, the Isabella tried the current, and found that it set north west, at the rate of seven or eight miles in twenty-four hours.

On Thursday, the 28th, we passed three icebergs, the height of the largest of which was measured by Lieutenant Parry, by taking the angle it subtended, and its bearings, at two stations, the distance between being ascertained by the patent log: its height was found to be fifty-one feet. Around these bergs were a great number of birds of different descriptions, some of which followed the ships for a consideraele distance.

During the night, and on the following morning, we passed several icebergs and smaller pieces of ice. One of those which we passed to-day (the 29th,) was the largest we had yet seen. On the top of it was an immense circular mass, resembling a tower, which appeared much whiter than any other part, probably from its being covered with snow. We had this day a good specimen of a northern summer, for it snowed and sleeted alternately during the whole of the day. This made the weather so thick, that a very vigilant look out became necessary to guard against running foul of the ice; and this danger would be still more serious at night, were it of any length. This is so far, however, from being the case, that last night, although we were then only in latitude 62° N., the twilight was so strong during the short time the sun was under the horizon, that any object of considerable size might be seen nearly as distinctly as in day-light, and to-night this refractive light will be stronger, and the night at the same time shorter, for at midnight we shall, if the wind continues, be as far as latitude 63° N.

Saturday, May 30th. The rigour of the climate still increases. Such parts of the rigging and sails as were wet yesterday, are to-day regularly frozen, and in some places adorned with isicles. The thermometer in the shade, at noon, rose no higher than twenty-eight degrees and a half; and the temperature of the sea-water at the surface was as low as the freezing point, notwith-standing the weather has been to-day much more agreeable than we have found it for some days past.

I had an opportunity, during the night, of observing the shortness, or rather the total absence, of darkness for the last twenty-four hours; for, having remained on deck until two o'clock of the morning of the 31st, for the purpose of being present at the measurement of a large iceberg which we then passed, I found that at midnight I could read the smallest print; and at half past one o'clock it was so clear, that I could read with the greatest ease the divisions on the sextant which was employed for taking the angle subtended by the iceberg.

The height of this iceberg was ascertained to be eighty-five feet, and its length five hundred and eighteen feet around its base. In some places, at a considerable distance from it, the sea broke with great violence, owing, no doubt, to some tongues which projected from it underneath the water. For a considerable distance to leeward of it there was a stream of small pieces of ice which had been detached from it.

Its figure was that of an irregular square, one side of which was quite perpendicular. From this side it sloped gradually towards the opposite side, where its height above the surface of the water did not exceed ten or twelve feet. I have observed this to be generally the form of the icebergs we have hitherto seen, that is, one side high and perpendicular, the opposite side quite low, and the surface sloping gradually from one side to the other. It is not to be understood, however, that this description is applicable to every iceberg: so far is this from being the case, that some of them do not answer in one single point to the form of those mentioned above. Several of them, indeed, have such fantastic shapes, that it would be a difficult matter to describe them correctly.

On Monday, June 1st, as for some days past, a great number of the whales called finners, (balæna physalus,) were seen. They derive their name from a fin on the back, not common to the black whale, (balæna mysticetus.) They are generally as long as, and sometimes longer than, the regular whale, but never so thick; and their blubber seldom exceeds five or six inches in thickness. From this circumstance, and the difficulty of killing them, which is sometimes a hazardous enterprise, they are seldom molested by the fishermen; but I understand that the natives of Greenland prefer their flesh to that of the black whale, and for that reason are greater enemies to them than the fishermen.

We observed several of them raise out of the water their enormous tails, with which they kept beating and lashing with great violence. On enquiring of those who had been employed in the Greenland fishery, what might apparently be the cause of these violent actions, we were told that they were owing to the congress or embrace of the two sexes. I have been informed that wherever these finners are met with in considerable numbers, a black whale is seldom or ever to be seen. With respect to the seals it is the reverse; for we saw them in greater numbers to-day than on any former occasion. It is not to be inferred from this, however, that the finners and seals associate together. I presume, on the contrary, that there is not any such alliance, although they happened to be seen together. We fired several times at the latter, but without success, as they instantly dived, whether struck or not. We were more fortunate, however, in procuring a few specimens of the feathered tribe : the weather being very fine, a boat was sent to an iceberg, around which we observed a great number of birds. Four of these were killed, namely, a loon, (colymbus troile;) a fulmar, (procellaria glacialis,) commonly called mallemuke, in which was found an egg without a shell ; a kittiwake, (larus Rissa;) and a Greenland swallow, (Sterna hirundo.) They were all excessively fat, the first two in particular, having each a layer of adipose substance, a quarter of an inch in thickness, underneath the skin. This is, as well as the thick down with which their breasts are covered, peculiarly well calculated to protect them against the rigour of the climate.

We were somewhat surprised to day on finding ourselves close to the iceberg mentioned yesterday, after beating about for the last twenty-four hours, and attempting to get to the northward. We passed as close to it again this day as the first time, notwithstanding we were at noon six miles to the northward of where we were yesterday, our latitude to-day being 63° 51′ 03″ N.; and on the preceding day 63° 45′ N. This would appear to controvert what has been said lately respecting a current setting to the southward and eastward round Cape Farewell. Be this as it may, I shall not fail to record facts, however irreconcileable they may appear.

On the following day, June 2d, we passed through several streams and patches of ice, amid which we saw numerous flocks of the birds the seamen call rotges, the alca alle of Penant's Arctic Zoology, It is a beautiful little bird, and agrees perfectly with the description given of it by that naturalist. We killed one, which we found to be very good eating.

It may not be improper in this place to give some explanation of the above terms of *streams* and *patches* of ice, together with that of such others as are usually employed in describing the different forms in which the ice is met with in these regions.

Those stupendous masses of ice fallen in with in Davis's Straits, and sometimes in Greenland, are called ICEBERGS, or ICE ISLANDS.

When a number of pieces of ice are collected together in close contact, in such a way as that they cannot be seen over from the mast-head, this is termed a PACK. When the collection of pieces can be seen across, if it assume a circular or polygonal form, the name of PATCH is applied to it; and it is termed a STREAM, when of an oblong form, however narrow it may be, provided the continuity of the pieces is preserved.

A FIELD is a continued sheet of ice, so large that its boundaries cannot be seen over from the ship's mast-head.

Pieces of ice of very large dimensions, but smaller than fields, are called FLOES. Thus a field may be compared to a pack, and a floe to a patch.

Small pieces which break off from the large masses are called ICE-BRASH, and may be collected into streams and patches.

Ice is said to be LOOSE, OPEN, or DRIFT, when the pieces are so separated as to allow a ship to pass through them.

A HUMMOCK is a protuberance raised upon any plane of ice above the common level.

A CALF is a portion of ice which has been depressed in the same manner as a hummock has been raised, namely, by pieces of ice mutually crushing each other.

The above definitions are taken from Mr. Scoresby's paper on polar ice. This gentleman also remarks, that fresh-water ice may be distinguished from salt-water ice by the black appearance of the former when floating in the sea, and its beautiful green hue when removed into the air. That such may generally be the case I am willing to allow; but I am inclined to think, that ice may be fresh without possessing either of these remarkable appearances, for some which we brought-from the iceberg we were at yesterday, was found to be perfectly fresh, although it neither looked black in the water, nor green when removed from it; but had, in both situations, rather a white or crystalline appearance, especially in the air, at the same time that the part of the iceberg which was above the surface of the water appeared to me to incline more to a blue than to a green colour.

It may, perhaps, be considered presumptuous in me thus far to differ from the authority of a man who had so many opportunities to make himself fully acquainted with the subject in question; but, with due deference to his superior knowledge, I must for the present beg to dissent from him with respect to the colour of fresh-water ice. Should I, however, hereafter find this instance to be only an exception to the general rule, I shall not fail to notice it as such.

During the forenoon of Wednesday, June 3d, we were obliged to stand to the eastward, in order to keep clear of the ice, which, to the northward and westward, we found scattered in patches and detached pieces, as far as the eye could penetrate. The distance, however, owing to the haziness of the weather, was not very great. Between twelve and one o'clock in the afternoon, we had the second view of the coast of Greenland, it having been indistinctly seen on Sunday last, the 31st of May, from the mast-head. On the present occasion, also, our distance from it was too great to afford us a distinct view of it, even at our nearest approach, which was before we tacked; for it was then estimated that we were distant from it fifty miles. How far this may have been correct I cannot pretend to say; but it appeared to be the prevailing opinion at the time, in both ships, the Isabella having then telegraphed that we were at that distance from the land.

It was not to be expected that much would be seen at such a distance; but we saw enough to satisfy ourselves of the barren and dreary nature of Greenland, for the eye, instead of being relieved, and the mind cheered, as they usually are on the first appearance of land, after some time having been spent at sea, were on this occasion appalled by the dismal aspect of snowy mountains, and black cliffs or precipices, on which neither snow nor ice could rest, owing to their steepness. We could neither perceive the summits nor the lower part of the mountains, the former being hid from us by a horizontal cloud or fog, which extended over the land as far as we could see, and the latter by the sea, owing to the distance we were off.

We ascertained that this part of the coast is laid down in the charts too far to the eastward; and, according to our chronometers, upwards of two degrees, unless, indeed, we were farther from it than we supposed ourselves to be.

On Thursday, the 4th, we had a better view of the land than on the preceding day, owing to the weather being clearer; while our distance from it was, I believe, nearly the same. The sky over the land being clear of clouds, we could plainly see the summits of the mountains for a considerable way inland. They appeared to be nearly of an equal height, and all terminating in acuminated points, separated from each other by small vallies, covered, or more properly speaking, filled with snow. Indeed, the whole face of the country, as far as we could see, was clad in the same manner, with the exception, as I have already observed, of the black cliffs and precipices which here and there protruded themselves to view.

The anniversary of our most gracious Majesty was not forgotten this day in our narrow circle; for his health was drank after dinner as cordially, and with as much glee, as at any table in his extensive dominions.

During the two following days nothing occurred deserving of notice. The wind having been directly against us, we have been forced to beat about nearly in the same tract between the land and the ice. The space between the former and the latter does not, I think, exceed eighty, or, at the most, ninety miles; for we constantly have a sight of each of them in the course of every twenty-four hours. Our approach to the ice is always known for some time before we reach, or even see it, there being invariably a kind of white fog, or glare, commonly called the ice blink, extending along the horizon in the direction in which it lies. This glare, or blink, generally assumes one particular form, which is that of a segment of a large circle, with its convex, or circular side, uppermost. The middle part is usually of the height of about five degrees. We constantly meet with small straggling pieces of ice for some miles before we reach the main body; and these continue to increase in number and size in proportion as we advance. I have observed also that, as we approach the ice, the birds are always more numerous.

From the sixth to the ninth we were engaged in working to the northward among the ice, which we found, on the latter day, to be so closely packed together, that it was impossible to get through it in any direction to the northward and westward, since it extended from the land right across to the westward, as far as we could see. After working about among the loose ice as far as we could well proceed, we at length drew in towards the land, and made fast* to a large iceberg, which was aground about three or four miles off the shore, or rather off some islands which lay between us and the main land. We were not long here before a number of Esquimaux came alongside of us in their canoes. Some of them had a few wild fowl, eggs, and seal-skins to barter; and others did not appear to have any other object in view beside that of gratifying their curiosity. The articles they appeared most desirous of bartering for, were clothes, iron, tobacco, and spirits; but, I believe, every thing was acceptable to them. They had, however, so little to dispose of, that but few of their wants could be supplied, unless this had been done gratuitously. They informed us, through the medium of their countryman, Sacheuse,† that not any of the fishing ships had as yet been able

---

* The usual way making fast to ice is to dig a small hole, or pit, in a convenient part of it, and into this is inserted a strong iron hook, commonly called an ice-anchor, to which a hawser or line is made fast.

† He is a native of this country, of South-East Bay, as I believe. He was taken to Leith about two years ago, by one of the fishing smacks belonging to

to get to the northward of this, on account of the ice. We have reason, however, to doubt this story, which is probably of their own making, with a view of detaining us here, in order to make their own market. The description of the Greenlanders, and of their canoes, given by different writers, accords so well with what we have hitherto seen of them, that any attempt of mine to describe them may, perhaps, be deemed unnecessary; but as I do not intend to confine my observations to those objects only which may appear to myself to be new, I shall here give a brief sketch of our visitors, and of their kajaks, or canoes.

The former appeared to be rather below the ordinary stature, but well proportioned, and stoutly built. Their faces were generally, but not invariably, broad, for one or two of them were observed with high cheek bones, and a long visage. Those who were broad-faced had always a flat nose and thick lips. Their eyes were small, and deeply seated, and their complexions bordered on a dirty olive colour. Some of them had long beards, and others looked rather naked about the face, as if the beard had been pulled out. Their hair was straight, coarse, and of a jet black colour. Their dress was made chiefly of sealskins, and consisted of a sort of frock and small clothes, with the hairy side of the skin generally outermost. The head-dress of the greater part of them was a Welch wig. Those among them whom I had an opportunity of seeing out of their canoes, had boots on, made of the same materials as the rest of their clothes, with this difference in the make of them, that instead of the hairy side being outermost, it was invariably the reverse. It appeared to me that both their feet and hands were small, in proportion to the other parts of their frame; but as I expect that we shall have yet many opportunities of seeing others in a more original state than our present visitors, some of whom I suspect to be of a mixed race of Danes and natives, I shall forbear entering into any minutiæ respecting them; and, indeed, were I inclined to give a more ample description of them, a single visit from a few would scarcely suffice to convey any thing like a correct idea of a whole nation.

Their canoes were made of seal-skins sewed tightly together on a wooden frame. They appeared to be in general between sixteen and eighteen feet in length, but very narrow, their breadth seldom, if ever, exceeding two feet. Their form

---

that port. The owner of the ship which brought him to Scotland seems to have paid him considerable attention, for he can now both read and write a little, and appears to have some idea of drawing. He speaks English tolerably well. He is with us in the capacity of an interpreter, but does not confine himself to that alone, as he works with the rest of the seamen; and, from what I can learn, is not much inferior to any of them as a useful and willing man on every occasion.

is somewhat like that of a weaver's shuttle, with the exception that both ends turn up a little, and the after end, I think, rather more than the other. In the middle is a circular hole, in which the Greenlander is seated, apparently with as little fear of being upset as if he were seated in the finest barge. Around the rim of this hole is fastened the tail, or lower edge of their seal-skin jackets, by which contrivance the canoe is completely water tight, even in the roughest sea. When they wish to rest themselves, they lean a little to one side, supporting themselves by the end of their paddle. I have observed some of them, however, balance themselves without this artifice, which is, perhaps, only necessary in rough weather. Their paddles are between five and six feet in length, small in the middle, at which part they lay hold of them, and broad at each extremity. By striking alternately on either side, they get through the water with a velocity equal to, if not exceeding, that of the swiftest row boat. Owing to their dexterity in managing their canoes, I believe the latter to be perfectly safe, notwithstanding a person unaccustomed to them would be in danger of upsetting. What we should be apt to consider as defects in these vessels in other parts of the world, are in this country essential qualities; I allude here to their lightness particularly; for whenever they are in danger of being beset by the ice, the natives have only to get upon it, and can easily carry their canoe on the shoulder, or even under the arm. Their being low in the water is another advantage, for they can approach seals and birds very closely without being perceived. All their fishing and fowling apparatus, namely, spears, harpoons, lines, and lances, are, with the exception of an inflated seal-skin, which is stationed behind, placed before them on the canoe. These, although simple, are well adapted to the respective purposes for which they are intended. The harpoon, which they employ for killing the seal, has the inflated seal-skin attached to it by a long thong. This buoy answers a double purpose, as it points out, in the first place, the course the animals take, so that they can be more readily followed, and, secondly, tends to exhaust them; since, whenever these animals are wounded, they instantly dive, and, by this constant struggle against the buoyant skin, in a short time fall a prey to their pursuers.

Having thus noted such few cursory remarks as I have been enabled to make on the skin-clad inhabitants of these dreary regions, I now return to other objects of more immediate concern. Notwithstanding we have been interrupted by the ice in the prosecution of our voyage, the time has not been uselessly spent, for several observations were made in the course of this afternoon, on the iceberg to which we are fast.

From these observations it would appear that this part of the coast is laid down in the charts nearly three degrees to the eastward of where it ought to be.

$\qquad \qquad \qquad \qquad \qquad \qquad \overset{\scriptsize\text{o} \qquad \prime}{}$

Longitude according to the charts 50 50 W.
Ditto.   Lunar   53 42 W.

$\qquad \qquad \qquad \qquad \qquad \overline{\text{2 54 W.}}$

$\qquad \qquad \qquad \qquad \qquad \overset{\scriptsize\text{o} \quad\prime\quad\prime\prime}{}$

Latitude by observation, at noon 68 22 15 N.
Ditto, by midnight altitude - 68 25 43 N.
Longitude by lunar - - - 53 42 00 W.⎫
Variation - - - - - - 67 32 00 W. ⎬ on the iceberg.
Dip of the needle - - - 82 30 00 W.⎭

Besides the convenience afforded by the iceberg for making accurate magnetic observations, inasmuch as the compasses were here free from any of that local attraction which had been latterly found to affect them so materially on board, it offered likewise a subject of speculation in itself; since, although it was not one of the largest in this vicinity, its size was such as to convey an idea, although imperfect, of the magnitude of some of the stupendous masses we daily see. Its height above the surface of the water was measured by a line, and found to be nine fathoms, (54 feet,) and the depth of water alongside was fifty-three fathoms, (318 feet,) which must have been its height under water, for it was fast aground : so that its entire height was not less than 372 feet. Its length and breadth were not measured; but I should imagine that its shortest diameter exceeded its height very considerably. The esquimaux said that it came hither last year; but whence they could not tell; it must certainly have come from some distance, for the low land hereabouts is not at all calculated for the formation of the immense masses of ice which are aground off this part of the coast. That a bold coast and deep water are essential to their formation, is obvious on several accounts. In the first place, they require deeper water to float in than we have found here ; and, secondly, they have in general, as has already been observed, one side quite perpendicular, which side I conceive to have been attached, when they were forming, to the surface of some lofty rock or precipice on the coast. And although we find them to consist of a solid, or compact ice, still it is evident that they were formed of sleet and snow, which fell on, or was drifted over some rock, or steep hill, that sheltered the accumulating mass. This, in all probability, requires several years to gather before it breaks off; and there is little, if any doubt, that it is formed in this manner, from the ice being perfectly fresh; insomuch that we filled some tanks with it this afternoon, in order to its being used for culinary purposes.

What suggested to me the idea that these icebergs are several years in forming, is, that we found on one of the sides of the one above-mentioned, a regular stratum, or bed, of sand and gravel, a few feet only above the surface of the water, besides a great number of large stones, one of which I conceive to have weighed nearly a ton, embedded in different parts. These stones, but more especially the layer of sand and gravel, 1 am inclined to think, had been carried down by a torrent of rain, in the summer season, from the side of the mountain or hill where the berg was formed. How far I am correct in the above conjectures, time will perhaps enable us to prove by observation, so as to put the matter out of doubt, if any such doubt exist. A piece of ice from this berg was cut into a perfect cube, the sides of which measured thirty-six lines. On being thrown into a bucket of salt water, of the temperature of $32°$, and of the specific gravity of $1026·9$, five lines, or nearly one-seventh part, remained above the surface of the water; which proportion agrees pretty nearly with the portion of the iceberg above, compared with that beneath the surface of the water.

During the night,* the ice began to close on the ships, so that we were obliged, on the following morning, June 10th, to cast off from the iceberg, and make the best of our way into clear water, if I may so call a sea every where interspersed with fragments of ice. For the first time we descried a black whale, the sight of which cheered up the spirits of our Greenland sailors, as much as the sight of game would those of a keen sportsman: they appeared to be all on the alert, and, as it were, anxious to go in chace.

On the following day we were gratified, for the first time since we left Shetland, with the sight of four ships, which, on our approach, we found to belong to Hull. One of them, the Venerable, which was boarded, had taken seven fish. They informed us that they had been as far north as Disco, to the westward of which they had found the sea open. It would appear that the frost had been very severe at the commencement of the season; for they had, to the northward, found the sea frozen three different times.

This day a large seal was shot from the Isabella. It weighed eight hundred and forty-six pounds. Its length, from the snout

---

* It is my intention to continue the usual distinction of day and night, notwithstanding the natural division does not at present exist here, for the sun never descends beneath the horizon. Last night, the latitude was obtained by its altitude at midnight.

to the tail, was eight feet, and its circumference, five feet four inches and a half. It was one of the species called phoca barbata. On examining the heart, the foramen ovale was found to be entirely obliterated. I have mentioned this, on account of a different opinion having been once entertained on this subject.

The seal in question had eight rows of pellucid white whiskers, whence it has been named. Fore flippers eleven inches long, six inches across the metacarpus, five fingers, the second from the front a little longer than the rest, resembling the human hand, except that it had five fingers, instead of four fingers and a thumb. Hind flippers sixteen inches in length, and, when spread, two feet across at the claws. There are five fingers, in length seven inches on these flippers also. Claws strait, brown colour beneath, black above. Upper lip rounded, fleshy, thick, extending beyond the lower one, which is thin and pointed. Iris hazel, pupil elliptic perpendicular, tongue fleshy, thick, slightly divided at the tip, upper surface papillous. Hair short, thick, and coarse, darkish grey. It was a male, and so young, that the teeth were scarcely developed ; but the rudiments of six front ones, in the upper jaw, were discernible. In the lower, there was room for four only, and they were not through the gums : two canine in each jaw. Upper jaw, three grinders produced through the gums ; lower seven. No external ears : orifice two inches back from the eyes. Skin and bones of the head and feet preserved ; flesh very black. The heart was eaten, and found sweet as that of a bullock, except the fat, which was rancid as train oil. About sixteen gallons of oil were extracted from the fat on it.

On Friday the 12th, in the forenoon, we made fast to another iceberg, being unable, for want of wind, to force our way through the ice. In a fissure, or small channel, filled with salt water, which ran for some distance across this berg, we found a number of clias, and another species of the order mollusca : one of them was of the shape, and nearly of the size, of a lady's thimble, and quite gelatinous, so that, when removed from the water, its sides collapsed. The other was nearly the size of an ordinary pea, and of a jet black colour. The clias were observed to feed on this latter species. Notwithstanding the diminutive size of these animals, they are said to constitute the food of the whale, and, for that reason, are all included, by the seamen, under the common denomination of " whale food."

In the afternoon, a light breeze having sprung up, we cast off from the iceberg, and began again to force our way to the northward through the ice. In the evening, the weather being clear and serene, both sky and water presented the most beautiful scene I ever beheld. The former, near the horizon, was interspersed with fleecy clouds, which decreased gradually in colour and den-

sity, according to their height, until, in the zenith, they disappeared entirely, and there the sky appeared of the most beautiful
cerulean blue. The water, on the other hand, or, rather, the ice
on its surface, presented a spectacle so superbly grand that I
know of no other scene in nature with which to compare it. Let
any one fancy himself situated in the centre of an immense
plain, extending farther than the eye can penetrate, filled with
masses of ice whiter than Parian marble, and presenting a greater
variety of forms than the most fertile imagination can conceive,
and as endless in size as in shape, from the stupendous icebergs
which stood at least a hundred feet above the water, to those small
fragments that were only discernible above the surface. I say,
let a person fancy himself situated in the midst of a chaos of
similar objects, and he will find it much easier to conceive than
express the grandeur of a such scene. The sun being at the time
a few degrees only above the horizon, added much to the magnificence of this sublime prospect.

Nothing particular occurred on the following day. We were
occasionally surrounded by streams and patches of ice, through
which we managed, however, to force our way. It was telegraphed to us, from the Isabella, to serve out a pound of Donkin's preserved meat to each of the crew to-morrow, as an extra
allowance.

On Sunday, the 14th, we got up to the Whale Fish Islands, the
Danish governor of which came off to the Isabella, and remained
on board some time. Between these islands, and the mainland to
the eastward, were seen some of the largest icebergs we had yet
passed. One of them was estimated to be upwards of two hundred feet above the surface of the water.

On the following day we passed several of the fishing ships,
some of them coming from the northward, they having been
unable to penetrate farther in that direction than the north end of
Waygat's Straits. Two of them which we boarded, namely, the
Everthorpe and Zephyr, of Hull, had taken five fish only, the
former two, and the latter three.

On Tuesday, the 16th, we passed a great number of very large
icebergs, some of them at least half a mile in length; and I
should imagine little short of two hundred feet in height. We
counted at one time not less than sixty-four from the ship's deck.
In fact, the whole of the horizon to the northward, appeared one
continued wall, or barrier, of ice, in one shape or other. We met
with some to day in larger pieces than usual, or that which comes
under the denomination of floes.

Mr. Muirhead, the master of the Larkins of Leith, came on
board of us this afternoon; and this afforded us an opportunity of
sending home some letters, or, rather, of putting them in a fair

way of reaching home, for it is not likely that he will leave this country for some time, having as yet procured only five fish. This gentleman proceeded last year as far north in this country as 75° 30′, and found the sea there quite clear of ice, from which circumstance he supposed that there must have been at least a hundred miles of clear water in that direction of him. He was not certain of his longitude at the time, but conjectures that he was about three hundred miles westward of the coast of Greenland, which part of it, laying to the northward, he found to be very low.

In the afternoon we hauled in towards Waygat, or Hare Island, on the north side of which we found between thirty and forty ships fast to the icebergs along shore. Such a sight, bursting suddenly on our view in these inhospitable regions, was highly gratifying, and at the same time afforded a striking proof of the enterprising spirit of our countrymen, in that particular branch of speculative commerce in which these ships are employed. All of those near to which we passed gave us three cheers, which were heartily returned. Shortly after we made fast to an iceberg on the north-east side of the island. Here we were obliged to remain for five days, owing to the ice being so close to the northward that it was in vain to attempt getting through it.

Our delay here was not, however, lost time, for several observations were made on shore, which could not possibly have been made on board ; such as the transit of the sun over the meridian, and the number of oscillations made by the pendulum of the astronomical clock, in the course of twenty-four hours, or, rather, from the time of the sun passing over the meridian one day, until its crossing the same the day following. The dip and variation of the needle were also ascertained very correctly by Lieutenant Parry and Captain Sabine, who passed three days on shore, in order to make these observations, sleeping in the tent in which the astronomical clock was set up. It was ascertained that the tide rose and fell ten feet on the third day after the full, or the time of the highest tide.

Within a few yards of the spot where the tent was pitched, were to be seen the ruins of an Esquimaux hut, which Sacheûse informed us was once inhabited by a very strong man, who was, on that account, much dreaded by his countrymen. Under a heap of stones, at a short distance from these ruins, several human bones were found : with the exception of one or two skulls, they were in a very decayed state.

Among the ruins themselves we found a piece of pot-stone (lapis ollaris.) We were given to understand that the natives make all their cooking utensils of this stone. The piece which was picked up by us, had been part of a jar, or pot, was very soft, and, on being scraped, greasy to the touch. Near the same spot was found a piece of bitumenized wood ; and on the shore, at a little distance, we met with several small pieces of wood, which appeared to have been a considerable time in the sea. What is most remarkable, they were all worm-eaten—a circumstance which would seem to prove that there are worms in the Frozen Ocean, as well as in tropical climates. As I believe this to be somewhat in opposition to the opinions of several able naturalists, it will perhaps require additional proofs, to demonstrate that this wood was eaten by worms in the artic regions.

On a small plain, by the sea side, about two miles to the southward of this spot, we came to the ruins of another hut. At what period these huts were inhabited is uncertain ; for Sacheuse's account of the strong man who dwelt near the place where the tent for the observatory was pitched, is traditional, he having been told the story by his father. It does not appear that any part of the island is inhabited at the present time ; nor is this much to be wondered at, for it is as barren a spot as nature ever formed. Such parts of it as are not covered with snow, present scarcely any thing but a rugged surface of rocks and loose stones. On the top of the hills there are indeed some plains, which may be more properly said to be covered with gravel than stones. On these plains a few small shrubs were observed, here and there, beginning to shoot up, but I seldom met with any which exceeded two inches in length. They were generally covered with a fine downy coat, which in all probability protects them against the vicissitudes of temperature that daily occur, and this to such a degree as would be apt to stagger the belief of those who have not had an opportunity of being an eye witness of them ; for at night, when the sun is low, it constantly freezes even the sea water ; while, in the day time, or when the sun is high, the thermometer in the sun rises as high as 84°. This was observed to be the case to day at noon, on board even ; but in the vallies on shore, where the reflection from the mountains is strong, it must be much hotter. In such parts of these vallies as were clear of snow, there were also a few vegetable productions, beginning to revive, such as short coarse heath, some dwarfish ground or creeping willow, with small tufts of grass in the moist or swampy parts of them.

The only four-footed animals which we saw on this island were two or three white hares, and a fox. The rigour of the climate did not, however, appear to stint the growth of these creatures, the former especially, for they appeared to me to be nearly double the size of our English hares. Bears are said to frequent this island, but none were seen during the time we were here. The track of one of them was, however, observed on the ice, or rather snow, between the island and the mainland.

The feathered tribe did not appear to be very numerous here. Those which we saw, were a few white Grouse, commonly called the Ptarmigan, Snow Buntings, Larks, and Snipes. It may not be improper to observe, with respect to the Grouse, that the male or cock only is white, for the hen is spotted or variegated like the English Partridge, and rather larger.

Although this island is but thinly inhabited by the animal creation, and steril with regard to vegetable productions, it abounds with a great variety of minerals : the most abundant, being that of which the fixed rocks are chiefly composed, is a stone of a blackish colour, very hard, and rather fragile. I suspect that it contains a portion of iron. The next, in point of abundance, is a black honey-combed stone, which has some appearance of volcanic origin. On the sides of most of the hills, a quantity of a dull whitish sort of a mineral was found. It was very brittle, porous, and light. Some detached masses of granite were occasionally met with, but no fixed rocks of that substance. We found a great quantity of Chalcedony on different parts of the island, but always in small pieces. Several other kinds of minerals have been found here occasionally ; but the most useful mineralogical production of this island is coal, a bed or stratum of which is found near the surface, and close to the shore, on the S. E. side. This coal is of a very inferior quality, and fit only to be used mixed with other coals. The fishing ships occasionally supply themselves with a little of it. Mr. Muirhead, master of the Larkins, of Leith, has taken a considerable quantity of it on board this summer. What I saw of it was of a slaty quality, and from what I can learn, this is its general nature.

Having now given a brief sketch of Waygat, or Hare island, and its productions, such of them at least as I had an opportunity of observing, I shall again resume my narrative of our proceedings on board.

Last night the floes of ice which blocked up the passage between the above island and the mainland, being observed to open a little in some places, we cast off from the iceberg, and began to force our way across the Waygat, as this passage is commonly called. At this place I conceive it may be about eighteen or twenty miles in breadth. When we had proceeded more than half way, we made fast, in the morning, to a floe, to give the people some rest, they having been up all night, towing and forcing the ship through.

We again cast off from the ice, and, by dint of hard labour and perseverance, succeeded at length in getting across ; and between seven and eight o'clock in the afternoon, made fast to an iceberg, about three quarters of a mile distant from the Greenland shore. Several of the fishing ships managed to break through at the same time, but the Isabella was not quite so successful, for the ice had closed round her during the night, in such a manner that she was not able to get more than half way over.

We found the land on this side to be much higher than that of Waygat island, but its general features, as well as the materials of which it is composed, as far as we have yet seen, appear to be nearly the same. Within view of the spot where we anchored, or rather made fast, several cascades of water fell from the rocky precipices with which this part of the coast abounds. On the beach, nearly opposite the ship, we found the spine and some other remains of the carcase of a large sea animal. It was supposed to be an Unicorn Narwhal, (Monodon Monoceros.) The greater part of it was buried under the ice ; enough of it however was seen to distinguish the element to which it belonged, for we found one of its flippers, which measured fifteen inches in length, and a foot in breadth.

The size of the spine was, indeed, sufficient to prove that it was not a land animal, each of the vertebræ being six inches in length, and between nine and ten in circumference. On the snow and land surrounding it, were numerous tracks of bears. A little way inland from this, we met with three other tracks, which resembled exactly those of an ox, and were about that size. We traced them for some distance along the snow. We were at a loss to conjecture what these animals could be ; but it is most probable that they are some kind of large deer. Where we saw their tracks they were going to the southward, at least as much so as the trending of the coast would allow. As we were struck with the magnitude of the print of the hoof, and the extent of the stride, we measured several, and the result is as follows :—

Breadth across the hoof.......................... 4¾ inches
Length of the hoof.................................. 4½ inches
Distance from the fore part of the
  one footsep, to the fore part of the
  fourth beyond it.......................... 8 feet, 10 inches

In the course of the forenoon of Monday, the 22d, the Isabella worked her way through the impediment of ice, and got over into clear water on the Greenland shore. It is particularly deserving of being remarked, that hitherto we have always found the sea clearer of ice near the shore, than further out at sea, which is rather at variance with the opinion of those who suppose the vicinity of land necessary to the formation of ice. But it may be asked, whether the loose floes and patches of ice with which the sea in these latitudes is almost covered, were not, at the time of their formation, united to the land ? May not the reflection of the sun's rays from the mountains tend, in a great measure, to dissolve the ice near the shore?

We got under weigh in the course of the forenoon, and having sailed along the coast to the Four Island point, we again made fast to an iceberg, it being impossible to proceed farther, owing to the closeness of the ice.

There is a small wooden house at this place, belonging to the Danes, who are at present gone to the northward to carry on the whale fishing; and we also observed the ruins of several Esquimaux huts in the neighbourhood of this house, or factory, as it is called; but neither a native nor a Dane was to be seen at the spot. It is situated in latitude 70° 40′ 00″ and latitude 54° 40′.

In the course of the following day, Tuesday, the 23d, we got a few miles further to the northward, by towing with the boats, which is, indeed, the only means that we have had in our power, for some days past, of getting on, there having been scarcely any wind. In the afternoon we made fast,·as usual, to an iceberg aground on the shore, and remained there for the night.

On Wednesday morning we again got under weigh, and towed along the land until we were interrupted by a floe of ice, which drifted in towards the shore with such velocity, that, had we not received timely assistance from three of the fishing ships, namely, the Thornton, Ingria, and Brothers, belonging to Hull, which fortunately happened to be close to us at the time, we should have been in great danger of being driven on that inhospitable shore. The good will and alacrity with which these ships sent their boats to our assistance, did them much credit, and entitle them to our sincere thanks and warmest gratitude. Not only on this, but on several other occasions, we had much reason to cherish these sentiments towards the ships engaged in the fishery, having uniformly experienced the most prompt and liberal disposition in them to lend us the most effectual aid in their power. One night, while we lay off Waygat Island, the iceberg to which we had made fast, in consequence of an unusual height of the tide, floated as it went adrift, and no sooner did they observe our situation, than their boats came to render us any assistance which we might require.

But I may say with great justice, that the same friendly spirit actuated us, no less than it was our duty to assist them in return. A few minutes after we had made fast, to day, the ship Egginton, of Hull, being driven aground by a floe of ice drifting against her in the manner above described, our boats were the first to assist her, and fortunately they, with those of the other ships, succeeded in getting her off before she had sustained any damage.

Nothing remarkable occurred on Thursday, the 25th, the

weather having been, as it had been for some days past, perfectly
calm, and the ice closed in all around us. A party of the officers,
as no attempt could be made to move, went on shore, but discovered nothing new, belonging either to the vegetable or mineral
kingdom.

On the following day, Friday, the 26th, in the forenoon, a light
breeze sprung up from the eastward, which soon made an opening,
by driving the ice to leeward, and we immediately got under weigh,
in order, if possible, to get across to the opposite side of the bay;
but in the midst of the attempt we were again stopped by the ice.
This bay is generally called North East Bay, and an inlet at the
bottom of it, Jacob's Bight. How far this inlet goes into the
interior is not known: none of the fishermen ever saw the bottom
of it, nor have heard that it has been seen. Some years ago,
a ship, called the William, of Liverpool, killed several whales a
great way within it; but, at present, like all the surface of the
sea in this quarter, it is covered with ice.

After beating about all night in search of, or rather waiting for
an opening, we found the ice so close in all directions to the
Northward, that it was in vain to attempt getting through it. We
therefore, on Saturday, the 27th, made fast to the land ice abreast
of an unknown island. In order to turn our delay here to 'as
much advantage as circumstances would allow of, several good
Lunars, Azimuths, and bearings of the land, were taken on the
ice alongside the ship, and the result of these observations was
as follows:

Latitude 71° 02' 22" N. Longitude by means of 8 Lunars, 54°
16' 30" W. and by Chronometer 54° 08' 00" W. Variation by mean
of four Azimuths 76° 02' W. the following bearings were taken
at the same time that the above observations were made: viz.

Western part of unknown island............S. 84° East.		⎫
Eastern ditto.................................... S. 10' East.		⎪
Centre of what appeared to be an island in the middle of Jacob's bight.	...S. 6° 30' W.	⎬ compass bearings
Western or outer land to the southward ... N. 83° W.		⎪
Ditto to the northward about Black Hook N. 22° 30' E.		⎭

In the evening we cast off from the ice, and kept sailing about
all night, ready to take advantage of an opening in the ice, should
any such occur.

On the following day, Sunday, the 28th, nothing occurred worthy of particular notice. Lieutenant Parry read prayers to the
ship's company, as he did indeed during the whole of the passage,
although I may have neglected to mention it regularly. I believe
that no more than one or two Sundays passed without his performing divine service; and its having been omitted on these days

was owing either to rough weather, or because all hands were necessarily employed, as was the case on the preceding Sunday.

On this day, and on the following, the weather was remarkably fine. With the exception of occasional light airs, a dead calm prevailed; and this was considered to be very much against us, as it was supposed that a fresh breeze for a day or two would break up the greater part of the ice with which we were surrounded, it being in that particular state which the seamen call rotten, that is, filled with cavities which had thawed away. It must certainly have been in a rapid state of dissolution, for the average temperature of the air for several days past, had been above 40°. The temperature of the sea-water at the surface was seldom, indeed, more than a degree or two higher than the freezing point; but still that part of the ice which was immersed in the water, was invariably found to be more dissolved than that which was in the air. In evidence of this fact, it should be noticed, that all the icebergs which were aground, had that part of them which was below high water mark, excavated or washed away for a considerable depth. This observation likewise applies to the floes and loose pieces of ice, their edges being constantly undermined, or washed away, in such a manner that some precaution was necessary in getting on them, since any one, by stepping on the edge, was almost sure of breaking it off, and thus, as did not fail to happen, get a cold ducking.

Notwithstanding the quantity of ice and snow which was dissolving daily on the surface of the water, and on the land, we did not find the specific gravity of the salt-water to be materially affected, it having been generally found to be about 1027, which is nearly the same as we ascertained it to be in the Atlantic ocean. The only way in which I can account for this is, that it was to be ascribed to the low temperature of the water, and consequently to its greater density, or, in other words, its increased specific gravity.

I neglected to mention that on Saturday last, the 27th, we received from the ship Middleton, of Aberdeen, a young seal of the species named phoca barbata. Of his habits little can yet be said: he has, however, manifested very evident signs of sagacity, considering his age. He had been but a few hours on board, when he found out the only holes in the ship's bulwark through which he could get overboard. These were two square holes, one on each side, cut for the purpose of passing through the end of the trough by which the water that was pumped was discharged into the sea. After these holes had been filled up with mats, he made several attempts to open them by the means of his fore flippers. He does not take any food unless forced upon him. Since he was caught, he has been fed with flour and water,

made into the consistence of thick gruel; but this appears to be
very inadequate to his support, as he pines away daily. He is
perhaps one of the most inoffensive animals ever met with, allowing himself to be handled like the tamest dog. Occasionally,
when disturbed, he makes a mournful noise, somewhat similar
to that of the crying of a young child. From having been so
long in confinement, it being nearly three weeks since he was
caught, he appears to have become quite helpless, even in his own
watery element; for on being let overboard yesterday, without
having a line fastened to him, he merely swam and dived for a
short time, and then came alongside the boat which followed
him, with a view, as was supposed, of being taken on board. In
diving he appears to make little if any use of his fore flippers;
and, when rising in the water, the hind ones seem to be equally
inactive; but in swimming both are used. In moving about on
deck, he does not make any use of his hind flippers, his motion
being a kind of hop or bounce, since, by bending his back, he
drags up the hinder part of the body, and then throws himself
forward by the means of his fore flippers. In this manner he
contrives to move along for a short space with about the same
speed as that of a person who walks at an ordinary pace. I suspect that his food, before he was caught, must have been chiefly
the milk of his dam, for whenever any one of the seamen approaches him, he begins to suck his trowsers. He passes the
greater part of his time in a state of somnolency, sometimes lying
on his back, but generally on his side.

The dimensions of this animal were as follow:

	Feet.	Inches.
Length from the snout to the tip of the hind flippers	3	2
Circumference of the thickest part of the head......	1	$2\frac{3}{4}$
Ditto round the neck when contracted	1	$5\frac{1}{2}$
Ditto round the body behind the fore flippers........	1	$10\frac{1}{2}$
Ditto round the body before the hind flippers........	1	$5\frac{1}{4}$
Ditto round the body where the hind flippers com- mence		10
Ditto round the fore flippers close to the body.......		7
Length of the fore flippers..............................		7
Ditto hind flippers.......................................		8
Circumference of the hind flippers close to the body		6
Length of the tail		$3\frac{1}{2}$
Thickness of the tail close to the body		$3\frac{1}{4}$

Teeth in the upper jaw... { 6 incisors,
　　　　　　　　　　　　2 canine, one on each side,
　　　　　　　　　　　　10 molares, five on each side.

Teeth in the lower jaw...... { 4 incisors,
　　　　　　　　　　　　　2 canine,
　　　　　　　　　　　　　10 molares.

Spread of the hind flippers ten inches, and of the fore flippers five inches.

The ears, or rather the foramina which led to the organ of hearing, for he had not any external ears, were situated about an inch behind the eyes, and of a size capable of admitting a large goose-quill. Nostrils situated like those of a dog. Strong bristles on the upper lip.

When lying still his heart pulsated at the rate of ninety strokes per minute. He weighed thirty pounds.

Before I conclude my remarks on seals, it may not be improper to observe that, within these few days past, several attempts have been made to get at those which have been seen now and then basking on the ice. From their having been observed at a great distance from the water, and having been frequently seen on the middle of floes several miles in circumference, we at first made ourselves certain of killing them before they could reach the edge of the ice. We soon learned, however, from experience, that their place of retreat was nearer to them than we were led to suppose; for we invariably found that they lay on the edge of a circular hole which went through the ice, so that, when we succeeded in getting within musket shot of them, they made but one hop, or bounce, and disappeared.

This day, Lieutenant Parry, with four other officers, two from the Isabella and two from our ship, went, by order of Captain Ross, on board the ship Eagle, of Hull, to inquire into the conduct of a part of the crew of that ship, who had, in the course of the last week, committed an act of the most wanton barbarity on shore at Four Island Point. This was nothing less than burning the house belonging to the Danish factory at that place.

On enquiring into the manner in which this disgraceful outrage was committed, it appeared, that two of the men had gone on shore without the knowledge of the master, who was in bed at the time, and, as it would appear, purposely with an intention to set fire to the house, for they had provided themselves with a tinder-box. The only excuse they had to make, when questioned as to their motive for so shameful a conduct, was, that the house had been plundered, and partly torn down, by other persons before they went on shore, so that they thought it nothing more than a piece of amusement, or, to use their own words, a piece of frolic, to give the finishing stroke to it, which they did so effectually, that scarcely a vestige of it was left unconsumed. The entire fabric being of wood, rendered its destruction complete. Mr. Bruce, the master of the Eagle, promised to acquaint the Danish Inspector-general, at Leifle Bay, of the whole transaction, in order to have the loss sustained, estimated, and paid for by those who did the mischief. I suspect, however, that the wages of two men will go but a little way towards defraying the damage done, as the value of a house in this country is much enhanced by the difficulty of procuring the materials of which it is made, at least the wood. It is to be hoped, notwithstanding, that whatever may be the pecuniary means of those who were concerned in burning this house, the matter will not be passed over unnoticed, to the end that others may be deterred from being guilty of so unwarrantable an act on a friendly nation.

On Tuesday, the 30th, Sacheuse was sent on shore to a small settlement which the Danes have on the south-side of Jacob's Bight, to inform the natives that we should be happy to see some of them on board the ships. In the afternoon seven canoes came off, and in one of them was a Dane belonging to the party to whom the house which was burned at Four Island point belonged. He informed us, that he was, together with his co-partners, to return in the course of a month to their winter habitation; but what will their astonishment be when they find the ashes only remaining where the building stood! At the place they now left, to visit us, they had procured three fish, and a considerable number of seals' skins. The former (the whales) belong to the Danes, who collect in the summer season, by the means of one or two small vessels, all the oil that is thus obtained at the different factories, or settlements, along the coast, and carry it to Leifle, their principal settlement to the northward, whence it is shipped for Denmark. The seal-skins being the raiment of the natives, and the flesh of these animals their food, these articles are resigned to them as their share of the booty.—I have said resigned, because the natives assist the Danes during the fishing season, and, in return for their services, receive from the latter their cooking utensils, fishing apparatus, and a variety of other articles, both useful and ornamental, such as knives, needles, looking glasses, beads, &c.

On the following day, July 1st, we had a visit from four of the Esquimaux ladies, and a young girl. They were from the same part of the land with the men mentioned above, and came off in a large boat, commonly called the women's boat, and, in their language, umiak. This boat was made of the same materials as their small canoes, namely, seal-skins sewed over a wooden frame, but was different in shape, being open above, like a common boat, and nearly of the same construction. This one was sufficiently capacious to carry ten or twelve persons with safety : there were, indeed, eight persons in at this time, besides as many dogs, and a sledge.

The men differed but little in appearance from those who came on board our ships on the 9th and 10th of the last month, so that little can be said of them in addition to what was noticed in the journal at that time. This being, however, the first time of our seeing any of the women, a few words respecting them may not be unacceptable. Their dress did not differ very materially from that of the men : the only difference, indeed, which I observed, was in the cut of their frocks, or jackets. Those of the women had a flap both before and behind, while the men's frocks were cut straight all round. These flaps were, together with the whole of the lower border of the frock, ornamented with a row of beads. The borders and breast were also trimmed with a narrow slip of red leather. The frocks of the men were, on the other hand, quite plain. The breeches and boots worn by either sex were precisely the same.

The women had not any head-dress, their hair being tied up in a neat tuft, or knot, on the top of the head. The men had caps made of dogs' skin ; but the other parts of their garments, as well as of those of the women, were of seal-skin. Two of the women had more the appearance of Danes than of Esquimaux ; and one of them in particular, had she been dressed in the European style, would have been considered a handsome woman. They were both considerably taller than the other two, who possessed all the characteristic features of the Greenlanders already described, namely, a broad, square, flat face, a pug nose, and small sunken eyes, with black, coarse, lank hair.

In their deportment both men and women appeared to be grave, modest, and unassuming, which justifies in some measure the compliment they pay themselves when approving the behaviour of a stranger. On any such occasion they are accustomed to say, " he is as modest as a Greenlander." Captain Ross gave them two rifles, and several toys, in exchange for the dogs, the sledge, and some of the women's dresses. The dogs are about the size of a shepherd's, or colly dog, with short erect ears, like those of a wolf. They are of different colours, some being black, others of a greyish colour, &c. Their harness consists of small thongs, one of which is passed round the neck, and another round the body, a little way behind the fore legs. To these are fastened the traces, which are made of the same materials ; and by these traces the sledge is drawn. The latter is made of firwood, very clumsily put together. It consists of two side pieces, the after ends of which turn upwards ; across these are laid narrow slips of board, at a short distance from each other; and between the upright pieces behind are a few thongs fastened in a reticulated manner, to support the back of the person who sits on the sledge. I did not take the dimensions of this one, but I should suppose it to have been between four and five feet in length, and three feet in breadth.

In the afternoon of the 2d of July, a breeze which sprang up from the south opened a passage through the ice along the north side of the bay. The zeal with which all the ships pushed through this opening, evinced the pleasure the crews felt on being releassd from the confinement in which they had been kept for some days past by the ice; for upwards of thirty sail of us were passing through the opening so near to each other, that the space occupied by the whole did not, according to my opinion, exceed a square mile. During the night we passed an immense number of icebergs, so close together, that any attempt to reckon them would have been impracticable; but even on the most moderate computation, they must have exceeded a thousand. Some of them were stupendous masses, and presented the most fantastic shapes.

During the whole of the following day, July the 3d, we were favoured with light breezes from the southward, which, together with an open sea, enabled us to make some progress to the northward. Our latitude at noon was 71° 30′ 13″ N. We were, generally speaking, between twenty and thirty miles from the land, which space we found to be pretty clear of ice, a few icebergs alone being occasionally met with. To the westward, as far as the eye could penetrate, the sea was equally clear. This enabled the fishing ships to spread themselves in all directions, some drawing in towards the land, while others directed their course to the westward, and a few still remained in company with us.

The land we passed to-day did not appear so high as that to the southward, and the tops of the mountains had a less rugged aspect.

On Saturday, the 4th, the sea was still clear of ice, as well between us and the land, as to the westward. In the afternoon we were abreast of Hope Sanderson, or, at least, of a high hill situated in the latitude in which the place so named is laid down in the charts. At this time we could see several islands to the northward, which we conjectured to be the southernmost of the Women Islands.

In the prosecution of our voyage this day we found the sea filled with what were apparently small particles of slimy matter of a yellowish colour. This was named by some of the seamen, "whales' food."

On Sunday, July 5th, in the morning, two of the natives of the Women Islands came alongside of us in their canoes. They informed us, through the medium of Sacheuse, that the sea was open to the northward. We were told still further by them, that, during the whole of the last winter, they had not had any ice on this part of the coast. It is difficult to reconcile this information with what we were told by the Danes to the southward; since either the weather must have been milder here than to the southward, or one of the parties must have misled us, either through inadvertence or design.

This afternoon we received two of the Esquimaux dogs from the Isabella. Not having spoken her since we left Jacob's Bight, until the present time, we were, in the interim, under considerable anxiety respecting the fate of Sacheuse, who happened to be on shore when we were on the eve of sailing from the above place. We were happy to find, however, that he returned to the Isabella before we sailed. His having been detained on shore so long, at the time alluded to, was occasioned by an accident which befel him, in consequence of his own folly, or, rather, of his ignorance; for having overloaded the musket he had with him, with a view of making sure of killing his object, or, to use his own words, " more powder more kill," it fractured his collar bone.

We passed, on Monday the 6th, several icebergs, one of which was aground in one hundred and twenty-three fathoms water. Its height above the surface of the water was ascertained by Lieutenant Parry, by trigonometrical measurement, to be one hundred and twenty-five and a half feet, which is nearly in the proportion of one to seven above the water, such as we found it to be by the experiment made on the cube of ice on the ninth of the last month, June.

Between these icebergs we found a considerable quantity of thin ice. In the afternoon the water had an unusual, yellowish, muddy appearance; but neither its temperature, nor specific gravity, indicated any particular change, the former being 35°, and the latter, 1026·6, which did not differ materially from what we had found it to be for some days past. Several of the fishing ships were still in company: one of them, the Royal George, of Hull, killed a whale in the evening.

During the forenoon of Tuesday, the 7th, we were in some measure interrupted by large floes of ice, round which we had to sail in various directions, in order to get to the northward. In the afternoon, we got as far as a small group of rocky islands, which are not laid down in any of our charts. They cannot be considered as belonging to the Women Islands, seeing that they are about fifty miles to the northward of that group. They were estimated by us to be about fourteen miles off the shore. On the mainland, opposite to these islands, stands a remarkably high hill, of the form of a sugar-loaf; and, from what I can learn, it is generally called by the fishermen, Sugar-Loaf Hill. Three bears were descried this morning on one of the floes of ice we passed: they were the first of these animals we had seen in this country.

At an inconsiderable distance to the northward of the group of islands above-mentioned, we had to encounter, on the following day, the 8th, a barrier of fixed ice, which extended from the land to the eastward, until it joined the main body of ice which ran up the middle of the straits, or, at least, which ran parallel with the land as far as we had yet gone. In consequence of this obstruction, we have done nothing this day but stand off and on between the mainland and the above islands. On standing close in to the coast, in the morning, we ascertained that the Sugar-Loaf Hill is situated on an island, or, rather, that it forms an island of itself.

In the afternoon, a boat was sent on shore to the southernmost of the outer group of islands, for the purpose of gathering eggs; but we found that all the nests which were accessible had been pillaged by the fishermen. On the south-east side of the island, a steep rock overhung the sea: here we met with a great number of nests, which I suspect to have been those of the lacus glaucous, commonly called burgomaster, as we saw a great number of these birds hovering about the face of the rock. The nests were made of lichen and dry moss. We likewise saw a great number of wild ducks on this island. Their nests were on the low land along shore, and consisted chiefly of feathers, which, from their colour, I apprehend to have been part of their own plumage. On different parts of this island we met with a considerable quantity of talc; and in several parts of the rocks along shore, numerous pieces of garnet were imbedded.

At a little distance from the shore, on the west side of the island, we came to one of the largest masses of quartz I ever witnessed. The other minerals of this island, such at least as I had an opportunity of observing, did not differ in any respect from those we found on Waygat island. There were very few plants of any description to be met with: indeed, the greater part of the surface of this island consisted merely of a confused heap of loose stones. On the west side, and not far from the mass of quartz above mentioned, we found a grave, which we conjectured to be that of an European, who had apparently been but recently buried.

From a manuscript copy of a letter of Mr. William Baffin, to one of the owners of the ship on board of which he acted as pilot in this country, we find that he makes mention of their having passed these islands, which they called "The Three Islands," a name not strictly correct with regard to their number, there being four islands in the outer cluster, besides two or three low islands between them and the mainland.

In other respects, however, Baffin was pretty correct, that is, with respect to the latitude in which they are situated; for he places them in 74° 04′ N., and we find the southernmost of them to be in latitude 74° 01′ N., which makes the others nearly in the situation in which he has placed them. Of the longitude in which they are, he makes no mention in the above letter, nor does he indeed notice the longitude of any of the places they named in this country, which certainly ought not to excite any surprize, when the imperfect state of navigation at the time he was here, upwards of two centuries ago, is considered. Indeed, his accuracy in obtaining the latitude so correctly, reflects no small degree of credit on his memory. He supposed the above islands to be only eight miles from the coast, which is very little, one mile only, more than half the distance we estimated them to be off; but as this is merely a matter of opinion, some regard is due to his judgment as well as to our own.

We made some progress to the westward, on the following day, among the ice, but found that the farther we advanced, the closer it became, insomuch that it was deemed prudent to return again towards the land. On the 10th, we observed that the ice had cleared away a little to the northward of the Three Islands.

On the 11th, the officers of both ships were employed in trying to ascertain the deviation of the compass, with the ship's head in different directions. This operation was performed in the following manner. The ship's head was brought to every second point of the compass, from west to south-east, the wind not permitting it to remain steady, for a sufficient length of time, at the remaining twelve points; and at each of the ten divisions, or second points, of that segment, the bearings of two fixed objects were taken by compasses placed in different parts of the ship. The fixed objects were, a certain point on the southernmost of the Three Islands, and a spot of snow on the top of the Sugar-Loaf Hill. Thus, by taking the true compass bearings of the objects on shore, the amount of deviation, with the ship's head in each of the above directions, was obtained. In order to give a better idea of this experiment than can be conveyed by words, a delineation of the diagram, No. I, made at the time, will be found opposite.

I am not aware that the above experiment has thrown much additional light on the subject of magnetism, since it is well known that the vicinity of iron constantly affects the magnet; and as not any part of the ship is free from this local attraction, it necessarily follows that the compasses will be more or less affected, according as they are removed from one part of the ship to another, or, in other words, in proportion as they are removed from, or towards, those places where the local influence is the greatest, from the quantity of iron collected. It is not to be expected, however, that the effects of local attraction will always be perceptible on the compass, although removed from one part to another. In the first place, there may be a local co-operation of forces, which may influence the compass in the same degree in two or more different places; and, secondly, the effect produced by local attraction may be so slight, that, as has already been noticed, it cannot be observed. This will unquestionably be always found to be the case in low latitudes, where the magnetic influence of the earth overcomes, in a great measure, all the power of local attraction, unless the compass be placed within the immediate sphere of action of the iron, or, to speak more properly, unless it be closer to any considerable body of that metal than compasses usually are, when employed for nautical purposes.

From the above experiments, Lieutenant Parry drew the following conclusions.

1st. The magnet deviates from its natural position, that is, from the position it would assume if uninfluenced by local attraction, with each alteration in the direction of the Alexander's head

2dly. That deviation is not equal, nor does it increase or decrease equally, in magnets placed in different parts of the Alexander, though a certain degree of regularity is observable in all.

3dly. The maximum of deviation in magnets placed in different parts of the Alexander, does not take place upon the same direction of the ship's head; for Kater's compass, elevated eight feet above the deck, and placed upon the spars which go across the ship, has its maximum of easterly deviation somewhere about east and east south-east; whereas the other Kater's compass, nine feet farther aft, upon the companion, has its maximum of easterly deviation somewhere between N. N. E. and E. N. E., making a difference of between five and six points.

4thly. The least deviation in magnets placed in different parts of the Alexander, seems also in very different directions of the ship's head; but it is worthy of remark, that the points on which the two Kater's compasses have their least deviation, are nearly at the same distance from each other, and on the same side as those on which they have their greatest, it being north in one, and W. N. W. in the other, equal to six points.

And 5thly. The points of greatest and least deviation in the magnet, on board the Alexander, are not opposite points of the

Plate I.

A DIAGRAM.

Exhibiting, at one view, the bearings by two different Compasses / on board·
his Majesty's Ship Alexander, of a distant object, upon every two points of the
direction of the Ships Head, from West to S.E. the wind not allowing the Ship's
Head to remain steady upon the other points, The Rhumb lines express the direction of the Ships Head and under each bearing is placed the amount of the
deviation, as compared with the true Compass bearing found on Shore. —
The true Magnetic bearings found on Shore were S‹.º 29´ E

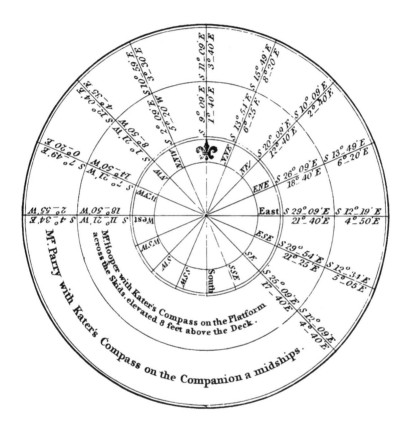

NB. The figures on the left side express the Compass bearings of the object
from the Ship and that to the right of each line what must be applied to
give the true Magnetic bearings of the same object as observed on Shore.

Example.

9º 09 E. is the bearings of the Object by Compass on board when the Ships
Head is North, and 1º 40´E. is what must be applied to give the true Magnetic
Bearings of the Same Object : Or in other words it is the deviation of the Compass on that Course viz. North. ———— It appears probable that an error was
committed in the bearings upon the N.E. course, and that the deviation should
be 12º 40´ instead of 2º 40´.

Neele & Son. sculpt 252 Strand.

compass, nor at right angles to each other, and consequently are not equidistant from the magnetic meridian.

During the three following days, the weather was remarkably foggy, and somewhat colder than usual, the whole of the rigging having been incrusted with ice, formed from the moisture of the atmosphere, by which the ropes were rendered stiff and uncomfortable to handle.

Wednesday, July the 15th. By applying the deviation, as ascertained on the 11th, the variation of the compass on board the Alexander, was found to be 82° west. This day we had a strong breeze from the north-east, which we expect will soon break up the ice, so as to enable us to get to the northward. Until the weather clears up, however, it is not likely that we shall make much further progress, for, should there even be an opening, we have barely a chance of finding it until some alteration in the state of the weather takes place. We were informed to day, by the ship Zephyr, of Hull, that the Three Brothers, belonging to the same port, was lost, a few days ago, in North-East Bay, by getting between two floes of ice, which closed on her with such violence, that she was cut right in two. Fortunately, however, not any lives were lost : the crew got immediately upon the ice, and were taken thence by some of the other whalers, which happened to be close by at the time. She had six fish in ; but not any part of them, nor indeed any thing else of consequence, with the exception of some of her boats, was saved. It appears that she was an old fir-ship ; but as we have not yet learned the particulars of the accident, it is impossible to say whether her loss was occasioned by the want of ordinary strength, or by the great weight of the ice. Let any one consider the violence of the shock which must ensue from the meeting of two floes, each perhaps several miles in circumference, and three feet thick, and these moving in contrary directions, at the rate of a mile, or of a mile and a half, an hour, and he will readily conceive the little chance a ship would have of withstanding the enormous pressure which would be upon her, were she to be caught in such a situation, that is, between two floes of the above dimensions, and in motion, as has been described. However incredible this description of the ice may appear, it is not an imaginary picture drawn by me ; for we have seen floes answering to the above description, as well in their size, as the rate at which they moved.

On the morning of the 16th, an opening having been observed in the ice, to the northward, we immediately availed ourselves of the opportunity of getting a little farther on, and found ourselves at noon, by meridional altitude, to be in 74° 24′ N., the farthest we have as yet been. We were detained, however, for two or three hours, by the meeting of two floes of ice, just as the Isa-

bella got through, and precisely at the time when we were about
to enter the lead, or opening, through which she passed. It is
deserving of remark, that we are frequently obstructed in this
manner ; for, whenever we have to pass through narrow openings,
which is very commonly the case, the water displaced by the
Isabella, causes such an indraught, that the floes often meet
before we get through, although, perhaps, we are not more than a
hundred yards astern of her at the time. From this circumstance,
I conceive, that if two or more ships are in company, working
through the ice, the one which sails best has, in this particular, a
decided advantage over the other.

This day we discharged Thomas Green, a seaman, into the
ship Equestris, of Hull, for a passage to England, on account of
his being subject to fits of epilepsy, accompanied by mental de-
rangement ; for during his last attack, he attempted to commit
suicide, from which he was prevented by some of his messmates,
who, fortunately, happened to be near him at the time. He succeeded, however, in making with his knife a deep incision across
his left wrist, making use, at the same time, of some expressions
indicative of his intention, such as, that he would die happy, and
other words to the same purport. He was a good willing man,
but had been observed for some time past to be very despondent,
on what account I have not been able to learn. In his stead, we
received a volunteer, named John Gordon, from the ship on board
of which he was sent.

On Friday the 17th, in the morning, a number of officers and
men from both ships, went in chase of a large white bear which
was on the floe of ice to which the ships were made fast. At the
time he was first seen he was not more than a mile from the
ships, and was then advancing towards them ; but immediately on
his observing that we were going towards him, he took to his heels,
and, notwithstanding his unwieldy form, and awkward amble, managed to travel faster than we could run. We pursued him to the
further side of the floe, which was about five miles from the ships ;
here he took the water, and by that means escaped, as we were not
provided with a boat to follow him farther.

This day we tried our ice saws for the first time, and found
them to be of considerable service ; for a neck, or isthmus of ice
about twenty-four yards in breadth, and four feet in thickness,
was cut through in the space of half an hour. This enabled the
ships to get into clear water, or, at least, so far clear that we advanced several miles to the northward before we had to encounter
any further interruption. It can hardly be said, however, that the
sawing of the neck of ice in question was the means of enabling
us to pass through ; for during the time our people were employed
in sawing, the hoes opened of their own accord, so as to enable

the Isabella to get through; but she had no sooner passed than they closed again, as happened yesterday, so that we had some difficulty in forcing our way after her. We found the ice here to be somewhat thicker than we had noticed it for some days past, being at an average about four feet in thickness. On its surface we met with numerous pools of fresh water, from which we filled some casks, and found it to be very good.

On Saturday, the 18th, in order to determine the proportion of saline matter in the floe ice, we dissolved a piece of it, and found the specific gravity of the water obtained from it, when at the temperature of 35°, to be 1001·27, which shows that it may be employed for any of the ordinary purposes of life, as well as that procured from the berg ice. The following is a detail of the particulars of this experiment.

From the floe of ice to which the ship was made fast, a piece was taken, and formed into a cube, the sides of which measured four inches, or forty lines. When this cube, or piece of ice, was put into salt water at the temperature of 32°, and at the specific gravity of 1025·8, the thickness of the portion of it above the surface of the water was six lines, or somewhat more than one-seventh of the whole mass. It would appear from this that the floe ice is specifically lighter than the berg ice: at least there is reason to draw such a conclusion from this single instance in which we tried them, on the 9th of June, and to day. May not this difference be ascribed chiefly to the difference of the specific gravity of the water in which the respective cubes were immersed? That it was partly owing to this cause, I think there cannot be any doubt. The floe of ice from which the above cube was made, was two feet ten inches in thickness; five inches of which were above the surface of the water.

From the freshness of this ice is it not reasonable to presume that, notwithstanding the floe is formed on the surface of the salt water, it still consists of what falls from the atmosphere? As far as my own observation goes, I am very much inclined to be of this opinion.

Nothing occurred on the 19th deserving of notice; the weather being very foggy, and our ships completely hemmed in by the ice, we were obliged to remain at the place where we made fast yesterday. We found the depth of water here to be two hundred and thirty fathoms, with a soft muddy bottom. The temperature of the water, at the depth of one hundred and ninety-seven fathoms, was 29⅝°, and at the surface 32°; that of the air being at the same time 37°. A whale passed us this morning going to the northward.

On the morning of Monday, the 20th, an opening having been observed in the ice, we immediately got under weigh, and by the assistance of the boats towing, proceeded a few miles to the northward, when we were again obliged to make fast to a floe, through the interruption of the ice, as had been usual.

We again got under weigh on the morning of the 21st, and as the ice had opened in different places, were enabled to get a little way to the northward. In the course of the day we passed the carcase of a whale floating on the surface of the water : it presented nothing but a shapeless mass, so that, even at the short distance we were from it, about half a mile, it would scarcely have been known to be an animal substance, had it not been for the disagreeable effluvia it emitted. A great number of glaucouses and fulmars were on and around it; but very few indeed of the latter species of birds were allowed by the former to sit on it. They had, however, an abundance of food, as well in its vicinity, as at a considerable distance from it, for we passed several pieces of crang, which is the name bestowed by the fishermen on the fleshy or muscular part of the whale after the blubber is taken off, long before we saw the carcase.

Notwithstanding the sea was comparatively open to the northward, we made but little progress on the following day, the 22d, owing to the calmness of the weather. The coast in this part appeared to be lined with islands, which were in general black and rugged; while that which we supposed to be the mainland was covered with snow, and its surface apparently more regular. Our distance from the land, however, being from sixteen to twenty miles, was too great to enable us to determine whether what we supposed to be islands were so in reality.

On Thursday, the 23d, the Royal George, of Hull, killed a whale close to us, while we were fast to a floe. We were thus enabled to have a good view of this enormous fish in its entire state, and, at the same time, to witness the whole of the operation of flinching. The following is an account of such remarks as I have been able to make.

This was a female fish, and of that size which is called middling, being neither very large, nor yet small. The length of her bone was ten feet and one inch. The bone here alluded to is the longest of the whale bones, by the length of which they judge of the size of the fish. The longest bone yet found, I understand to have been fourteen feet in length. Different parts, or organs, of the whale struck me as being very disproportionate : her head appeared to be upwards of one third of her whole length. The eyes, including the tunica sclerotica, or hard fibrous case in which they are inclosed, were only three inches in diameter; and the balls of the eyes did not exceed those of an ordinary-sized bullock. They consisted, like the human eye, of a crystalline lens, and vitreous humour; the pupil was elliptical, and of a darkish colour.

The teats, or nipples, were two in number, and were also much smaller than might have been expected, considering the size of the fish, being only about an inch in length, and the same in diameter : they were situated one on each side of the parts of generation. The external orifice of these parts did not appear to be above fifteen inches in length : they were situated near the after part of the abdomen, or where the body begins to taper suddenly towards the tail.

The whale has two fins only, which are, however, of an immense size ; they are situated on each side of the body, a little behind the after part of the mouth, or where the jaw bones terminate. The tail is proportionably large, and is placed horizontally. It does not, any more than the fins, resemble in texture that of other fish ; it being covered, in common with them, with skin of the same colour, consistence, and thickness as that on other parts of the body. Thus both fins and tail differ internally but little from the blubber on the other parts, being only somewhat more cartilaginous.

The skin of the whale which is the subject of these remarks, was in general between three quarters of an inch and an inch in thickness ; it was, with the exception of a small part of the lower lip, which was white, of a jet black colour, soft, and very easily torn, or cut. Instead of its being arranged in longitudinal layers, like the skin of most other animals, that of the whale is formed of vertical fibres, resembling a transverse section of a piece of wood. Next to the skin, is the blubber, or that part which subjects this inoffensive fish to such persecution. This oleaginous layer is of a different thickness on different parts of the body ; and in the present instance its thickest part was a foot. Beneath the blubber there is a thin layer of white, stringy, or fibrous substance, much tougher than the former substance ; and under this is the crang, or muscular part of the fish, which is of a very dark colour, and so soft and tender that it may be easily torn asunder by the hand.

The whale-bones are situated in two rows, in the upper jaw, occupying precisely the situation of the teeth of other animals, with this exception, however, that, instead of being fixed in each side of the jaw, they are attached to a semicircular bone, called the crown bone, which runs in a longitudinal direction along the middle of the upper jaw, or crown of the head. They are of unequal lengths, being longest about the middle of the row, and becoming shorter towards either extremity. I am uncertain as to the number of them on each side ; but I should suppose there must be at least three hundred of them in each row. There is an idle story among the fishermen that there is a bone for every day of the year ; but I suspect this to be nothing more than a vague tradition handed down from the one to the other, for the sake of establishing a marvellous coincidence between two things which certainly have not any relation to each other. I am, indeed, of opinion, that whales have a greater or less number of these bones according to their age, for, in this fish there were several blades of whale-bone only just protruding through the gum. They are situated at the distance of about three-fourths of an inch from each other, and are fastened in a soft elastic substance, which is called the gum. The interior edge of the whale-bone is covered with hair, or a sort of fibrous substance resembling it, which prevents the tongue from being injured by friction against the edge of the bones.

The tongue is an immense mass of soft substance, partly blubber, and partly crang, intermixed. Near the tip it consists chiefly of the former, for which reason a considerable portion of it is taken in with the blubber. I should imagine that the tongue of the above fish must have weighed between four and five tons. The nostrils, or blow holes, of the whale, are two in number, situated in the crown of the head ; their form somewhat resembles that of an italic *S*, and they are situated, relatively to each other, in a manner similiar to that of the openings in the upper part of a violin.

The length of this whale was estimated to be between fifty and sixty feet, and, at the thickest part, about the same in circumference; but as not only this, but every other dimension which has been given, were, with the exception of the length of the whale-bone, the thickness of the blubber, and the size of the eye, founded on a simple estimate, and not on actual measurement, it is not to be expected that what has been said on that head is to be relied upon as being strictly correct. It was supposed that the fish in question would yield between fourteen and fifteen tons of oil.

The operation of flinching is nothing more than cutting the blubber off the fish in large square pieces, a broad belt of it, which they call the " cant," being left for the purpose of turning the fish round as they proceed with the operation.

Several azimuths were taken this afternoon on the ice; and by these the variation appears to be 89° west, which is rather unaccountable, as it was found yesterday to be only 87° west ; we have, notwithstanding, altered our situation since that time not more than a few miles. Our latitude by meridian altitude at noon, was 75° 04′ 37″ north, and longitude by lunar observation 60° 05′·45″, and by chronometer 60° 09′ 52″ west. The magnetic dip was 84° 25′ 06″ west. If the variation found to day is to be depended on, we must be pretty near the parallel of latitude in which the magnetic pole is situated; but. I believe, there are some doubts existing respecting the azimuths.

We discharged James Curran this afternoon into the Royal George, from which we received a volunteer in his stead; but it having afterwards appeared that the same man had been the night before on board the Isabella, to make a tender of his services, Captain Ross ordered him to be sent on board that ship. This was accordingly done; but we received another man, named Marshall, from the Royal George, in the place of Curran.

On Friday, the 24th, we discharged two more of our indifferent hands, viz. Christopher Trew, and Henry Wright, into the ship Everthorpe, of Hull, from which we received two volunteers, named Thomas Snow, and Thomas Wyrell. After having proceeded a few miles to the northward, we were, as usual, stopped by the ice. In this particular spot, we were surrounded, in the evening, by more whales than we had seen since we came into this country, four or five of them being often observed blowing close to each other. The Dexterity, of Leith, killed three during the night, and struck another from the ice, which, however, got away. Certainly, had there been more ships in this water, a great number of fish might have been killed; but the Dexterity, Bon-Accord, Royal George, Equestris, and Everthorpe, are the only ships which have as yet got so far as this to the northward. Indeed, the former is the only ship which has penetrated as far as where the fish appear to be most plentiful. One or two of the others, however, in the course of the afternoon, killed some fish.

On the following day we discharged another of our men, William Parkinson, into the Dexterity, from which we received a smart looking young lad, of the name of Bruce, in his stead. I conceive that we are now well manned, that is, if our new men should be equal to the rest.

While the crews of both the ships were on the ice to day, tracking the Isabella along between two floes, one of the most ludicrous scenes occurred that I have witnessed for some time past. It may be, perhaps, considered too frivolous to be mentioned; but from the laughter it excited at the time, I cannot refrain from introducing it. One of the men belonging to the Isabella, who plays the violin, was, as usual, giving the men a tune on that instrument, to cheer them along in their laborious task, when all on a sudden, in the middle of a lively air, both the fiddler and the fiddle disappeared, he having dropped through a hole in the ice. The consternation of all hands, at the first moment, on finding the music so suddenly stopped, and the burst of laughter which ensued on discovering the cause, may be more readily conceived than described. The poor fellow got up again without sustaining any other damage beside a cold ducking and a wet fiddle.

Several officers from both ships went in the afternoon to a small island which lay a few miles off the coast. They found on it the ruins of an Esquimaux hut, near to which they picked up a human skull, and some pieces of bone which had apparently been the heads of darts or spears. On this island they shot several birds of a species which appears to have been hitherto quite unknown, not only to naturalists, at least to Linnæus, Pennant, Montagu, and some others, whose works we have on board, but also to Sacheuse, who tells us that he never saw any of the kind before. They have strong characteristic marks: the bill, which is an inch and three-tenths in length, is black, and tipped with yellow; the upper mandible a little hooked at the end; the inside of the mouth red; the head, and about an inch of the neck, of a lead colour, terminating with a black ring; the remainder of the neck, lower part of the body, and tail, snow white; the back and coverts of the wings of a pale grey; five outer primaries, black tipped with white; the remainder and secondaries pure white; under part of the wings white; legs black; feet webbed; length, fifteen inches; extent, two feet seven inches.

During the whole of Sunday, the 26th, we were fast to a floe of ice. The weather was extremely mild, and perfectly calm. To the northward and westward the ice was still close.

On the following day we were employed in making another series of experiments for the purpose of obtaining the deviation of the magnetic needle. They were performed, as before, by taking the bearings of a distant object with the ship's head in different directions. The result of these experiments will be seen in the engraved diagram, No. 2.

On the morning of Wednesday, the 29th, the wind having sprung up from the eastward, cleared away the ice a little, so as to enable us to get on: it being, however, against us, we were not enabled to make any considerable progress. At noon we were in latitude 75° 29' north. In the forenoon we passed a remarkable looking hill, not unlike a thumb in its appearance. We cannot suppose it, however, to be what the fishermen call "the Devil's Thumb," for they seldom, I understand, come so far as this to the northward. It should, besides, be noticed, that on the 22d of this month, being then in latitude 75° 03', we passed a hill which also resembled a thumb, and which is most likely to be the one called, by the fishermen, "the Devil's Thumb." There are apparently a number of islands along the coast here, as well as to the southward: they, that is, if they really are islands, for of this we are uncertain, being

Plate II.

A DIAGRAM.

Exhibiting the Second Series of Experiments on board the Alexander, for the purpose of finding the deviation of the Magnetic needle July 27ᵗʰ 1818. Latitude 15°.25'30"11 The true Magnetic bearings of the distant object being South or 180°."

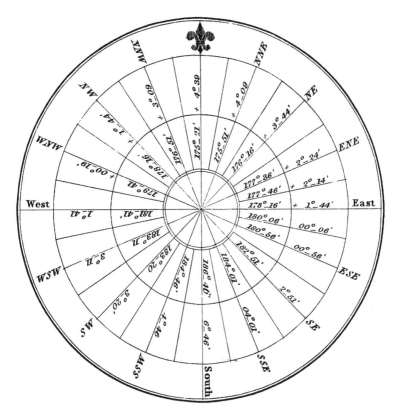

N.B. *The inner Circle denotes the Magnetic bearings of the object as taken on board on that direction of the Ships Head. And the Outer Circle the amount of the deviation.*

N.B. *The Rhumb lines express the direction of the Ships Head, mark'd on the outer Circle, The second Circle is the correction necessary to be applied to the bearings on each course in order to obtain the true Magnetic bearings: The third Circle contains the Actual bearings of the distant Object upon each direction of the Ships Head by a Kater's Compass placed upon the Companion a Midships.*

Neele & Son. sculp. 352 Strand.

shut out from the land by what is called the land ice, are in general more rugged than the main land behind them, and for the greater part clearer of snow, some being, indeed, nearly black; while that which we conceive to be the main land, is almost entirely covered with snow ; insomuch that, were it not for the black cliffs along shore, it might be taken for a solid continent of snow. In reality, for ought we know, a considerable part of what we regard as land, may be nothing but snow and ice. It may be presumed, I think, without any risk of making a wrong estimate, that the quantity of snow and ice in this country would require several years to dissolve, allowing the temperature of the air to be never below what it is at present. At noon, the Mercury in the shade stood at 33½° of Fahrenheit. I do not mean to say, however, that there is an annual increase of snow and ice in these regions ; for I conceive that such an idea would ultimately lead to an absurd conclusion. I shall therefore give it as my humble opinion, that in these climates, as well as in other parts of the world, there is a difference in some seasons ; so that the snow and ice which continue to accumulate for several winters, may be destroyed by one, or by several warm summers which may happen to follow in succession.

The land begins to trend here considerably to the westward, its northern extreme bearing N. by E. or N. N. E. by compass, which, allowing for variation, as observed on the 23d, will make its true bearings nearly W. by N., or W. N. W.

On Friday, the 31st, we got into a large sheet of clear water, in which we saw an immense number of whales. One of these was killed, in the course of the afternoon, by the Isabella's boats and ours : it was a male fish, forty-six feet in length, with a breadth of tail of fifteen feet, and length of bone, that is, of the whale-bone, nine feet six inches. It is unnecessary to enter into a lengthened detail respecting this fish, as it did not differ materially, except in size and sex, from the one we saw alongside the Royal George, and a particular description of which was given under date of the 23d instant. A difference was, however, observable in the colour of the lower part of the body, which, instead of being black, like that of the female fish, was of a mottled white.

The crews of both ships were, on Saturday, the 1st of August, employed for some time in flinching the fish taken yesterday. The number of whales around us this day, exceeded whatever we had seen before. It being calm, the noise of their blowing resembled, in some measure, the sound of distant artillery. They were generally about the edge of the land floe, from beneath which they appeared to come out to breathe. Sometimes a dozen of them might be seen at once, blowing so close together, that the spouts of water which they threw up, resembled in some measure the smoke from a small village on a calm day. Three or four of the fishing ships reached so far to the northward to day, as to be within sight of us. The Bon Accord, of Aberdeen, and Ever-thorpe, of Hull, were indeed, in the afternoon, within eight or nine miles of us. As a proof of the vast number of whales by which we are surrounded at present, each of these ships killed four to day; and had there been twenty ships here, I am per-suaded that each might have killed as many.

Within this day or two we have seen a great number of ivory gulls, (larus eburneus) a dozen of which were shot by me this afternoon. This is a very handsome bird; and it appears to me that, from the whiteness of its plumage, it may more properly be called the snow gull, than the ivory gull.

On the following day we found the land to trend still more to the westward, the northern extreme bearing N. by W. by com-pass, which, allowing for variation, will make it W. by S. By Azimuths taken on the ice, the variation was found to be 90° 25′ W. It is worthy of remark that the Azimuths taken on the ice on the 23d ultimo, were, as was then expected, erroneous; for on the 30th the variation was found to be only 87° 23′ W., and we were then upwards of twenty miles to the northward of where we were on the 23d. The error above mentioned is supposed to have arisen from the compasses being attracted by the Isabella at the time of observation. If such be really the case, it is one of the strongest proofs we have yet had of the effect of local attraction, the Isabella being at least a hundred yards from the spot where the compasses were placed. Our latitude to day at noon was 75° 48′ 36″ N., and longitude 62° 35′ W. The dip of the needle on the ice was 84° 44′ 55″.

We estimated the land to be about twenty-five miles from us at the time these bearings were taken, the whole of the intervening space being covered with land ice. We had not any interruption from the ice; but throughout the whole of this day the wind was so light, that we made but little progress. The weather was ex-tremely fine, and the sky perfectly clear and serene. We saw but few whales; but the number of rotges (alca alle) by which we were surrounded, was such as in a manner to exceed all belief. I may venture to say that since the morning we have seen several millions: they were generally in immense flocks flying to the westward, or along the edge of the land ice. We passed myriads of them also on the water, and resting on pieces of ice, some of which were literally covered with them.

On Monday, the 3d, we were favoured with a light breeze from the southward and eastward, which enabled us to run a con-siderable distance along the coast to the westward; but in the

afternoon our progress was stopped by the ice, to which we made
fast, in the hope of soon finding an opening through which we
might pass, as the breeze still continued.

After waiting, however, until the noon of the following day,
we found that there was not any immediate prospect of the ice
opening in the direction in which we were desirous to proceed,
namely, along the coast. The wind being from the southward,
instead of clearing away the ice, forced it in towards the land,
which in this part was nearly East and West. (true.) If there was,
indeed, any difference, the trending was rather to the Southward of
West. Shortly after twelve o'clock, A. M., we cast off from the
ice, in order to get to the Southward, where there appeared to be
some lanes of clear water among the floes, which were then
drifting pretty fast to the Westward, or along the coast. Before
we made sail, the observations and bearings which here follow,
were taken on the floe to which we were then fast.

	°	′	″	
Latitude by meridian altitude at noon	76	00	04	N.
Longitude by Chronometer	64	48	13	W
Variation by Azimuths	90	46	00	W.
Dip of the Needle	84	52	06	W.

It is necessary to observe that the places, the bearings of which
were taken as beneath, were supposed to be Baffin's Cape Dudley
Digges, and the island which he describes as being situated at
the entrance of sir John Wolstenholm's Sound. Although the
relative situation of the places in question agrees tolerably well
with the description given by this navigator, of the above mentioned cape and island, still there is such a wide difference in the
latitude, that we can hardly admit them to be the places so
named by him; for he lays down Cape Dudley Digges in latitude
76° 35′ N., which is at least twenty-six, or twenty-seven miles to
the Northward of that which we were led to suppose to be the
same, seeing that, by making the most ample allowance for the
distance between it and our ships, we cannot estimate its latitude
higher than 76° 8′ or 9′ N.

Instead, however, of attempting to reconcile this disagreement
in point of latitude, I shall give the bearings which were taken
this morning. " The point, (Baffin's island) off sir Dudley
Digges' Cape, S. 17° 47′ E. ; the cape itself being seen over
the above point, or island. S. W. point of the island in the middle of sir John Wolstenholm's Sound, N. 14° 04′ W. Eastern
extremity of the land, very distant, S. 5° 29′ E. (compass bearings) variation 90° 46′.

We made very little progress during the two following days,
owing to the ice having closed around us in all directions. On
Thursday the 6th, in the afternoon, it began to open a little to
the northward, that is, between us and the supposed Wolsten-

holm's Sound. We did not lose any time in taking advantage of
these openings ; but the wind being very light, we did not get to
any great distance ; and, indeed, the small advance we made was
chiefly accomplished by towing with the boats, or tracking along
the edge of the ice.

We have latterly experienced much obstruction from the young,
or what is commonly called the bay ice. It forms during the
night, that is, between ten o'clock, P. M. and two in the morning. We find it sometimes three-fourths of an inch in thickness,
and, comparatively speaking, so tough, that it stops the ship's
way, unless we have a good breeze of wind, with which, for some
time past, we have been but seldom favoured. The number of
little auks, or rotges, seen every day, is incredible. During the
two days last past we have killed about two hundred and fifty of
them, which have been served out to the ship's company, who
relish them very much—this is, indeed, not surprising; since I
am persuaded that, if they were to be properly dressed, they
would be considered as a savoury dish at the tables of the greatest epicures.

On Friday, August the 7th, both the Isabella and our ship
received considerable damage, by getting jammed between two
immense floes of ice, which were passing each other with a velocity of at least two miles an hour. In the narrow lane between
them, the two ships at one time came unavoidably alongside of
each other ; and in this position they were, for a short time, so
violently squeezed together, that little less than their total destruction was apprehended for a few moments. Out of this
perilous situation, however, we extricated ourselves, without
suffering so much as was dreaded, although not without considerable damage ; for we not only lost our small bower anchor, the
shank of which was broken off close to the stock, but three of the
main, two of the fore, and one of the mizen, larboard chain
plates were carried away by the stock of the Isabella's small
bower anchor. Our larboard-quarter boats, davids, a spare jib-
boom, cross-jack yard, and a part of the larboard bulwark, were
also carried away by getting foul of the Isabella. She suffered
some damage also, although I believe not quite so much as we
sustained : her most material loss was that of one of her boats,
which was destroyed between the two ships.

Even after we had succeeded in extricating ourselves from the
above floes, we were far from being clear of danger ; for the ice
ran with such velocity, that, during the whole of the afternoon,
and ensuing night, we were kept in a constant state of anxiety
for the safety of the ships. About midnight, the crews of both
the ships began to saw a dock in one of the floes ; but, owing to
the thickness of the ice, which was seven feet, they made so

little progress, that the undertaking was abandoned after two hours' labour. Independently of this, that part of the floe on which they were at work, had, by this time, drifted very close to some icebegs to leeward, insomuch that, if the dock had been cut, it would not have been safe to get the ships into it, under these particular circumstances.

On the morning of Saturday, the 8th, between four and five o'clock, a considerable space of clear water was made around the ships, by the opening of the floes. This favourable change relieved our apprehensions for the present: the ships were got under sail, and two watches of the ship's company allowed to go to rest, of which they had much need, all hands having been almost constantly on deck for upwards of twenty four hours, and exposed, during the whole of that time, to the most inclement weather we have experienced since we came into these regions; for it blew very fresh, and snowed without intermission, during the whole of the time. In fact, it was, in every respect, what would be considered a severe winter day in England.

The weather having cleared up in the course of the morning, we found ourselves abreast of the island at the entrance of the supposed Wolstenholm's Sound. In the afternoon several of the officers of the Isabella went over the ice to this island, but did not meet with any thing to compensate them for so long a walk, it being at least five miles from the ships. Like several others on which we have landed, it appears to have been once inhabited; for they found several graves on it, and a piece of stick similar to those which agreeably to the information of Sacheuse, are used by his countrymen for stirring the oil and lichen in their lamps.

The ice being close to the westward, we made fast, in the afternoon, to the land-floe; and this afforded us an opportunity of procuring a few fresh meals for the ship's company, we having, in the course of two or three hours, killed three hundred rotges. To give some idea of the immense number of these birds found here, I shall mention one circumstance, which will enable the reader to judge better of the prodigious flocks of them flying about, than any description of mine could convey. It is that not less than fifty-six birds were killed by two discharges of a pair of fowling-pieces, thirty-two of them having been brought down by a single discharge. For some days past, I had observed that many of these birds had a swelling or protuberance, in the under part of the neck. On examining several of them to day with this goître, I found it to be a small bag, or repository, beneath the tongue, and which was filled with small red shrimps.

On Sunday, the 9th, in the morning, just as we were casting off from the floe, three sledges, drawn by dogs, were observed driving along the ice, towards the ships. There were four per-

sons in them, two being in one sledge. After gazing for a little
time at the ships, they fled with as much speed as if they had
been pursued. They did not approach sufficiently near to enable
us to form any thing like an accurate judgment of their appearance; but several on board were of opinion, that they were
larger men than those we saw to the southward.

In the hope of enticing them to return, provided we should
be obliged to make any further stay at this place, or at any event,
with a view to spread among the natives along the coast a favourable report of us, Captain Ross put several strings of beads
round the neck of one of the dogs we had procured from the
Esquimaux in Jacob's Bight, and left the animal on the floe of
ice from which we had cast off. One of the stools on which the
compasses were placed, when taking observations on the ice, was
also left with strings of beads on it. As the ships sailed imme-
dietely after this was done, we could not assure ourselves whether
they returned to pick up these articles or not; but it is probable
that the dog would, after a time, find out their habitations, and
by that means lead to a discovery of the rest of the presents left
for them. However, after working to the westward the whole
of the day, along the edge of the land ice, we found, in the
evening, that there was not any passage round the point which
forms the south-western side of the supposed Wolstenholm's
Sound. We therefore returned to the place we had started from
in the morning, and there found the poor dog, together with the
other presents, which had been left untouched. They were all
taken on board; and about midnight we again made fast to the
floe, nearly at the spot from which we had started in the morning.

On the following morning we observed four sledges, drawn by
dogs, coming towards the ships. In order to induce those within
them to approach, Sacheuse was dispatched with presents to
meet them. On his coming within a short distance of them, both
parties stopped, apparently apprehensive of each other, Sacheuse
in the mean time holding up the articles he had with him, with
a view of convincing them of his pacific intentions. At length
both parties mustered a little courage, and ultimately met; but
before the natives allowed Sacheuse to approach them, they cau-
tioned him to be on his guard, as they had the means of killing him,
brandishing, at the same time, their knives, no doubt with a view
of showing him how formidable they were. After some con-
ference, he at length succeeded in convincing them that not any
harm was intended, and assured them that they might come on
board the ships with perfect safety, which, after some hesitation,
they consented to.

On their coming on board the Isabella, they appeared to be
for some time lost in astonishment at the novelty of the scene by

which they were surrounded, every object, in reality, attracting their attention. The height of the masts, in particular, seemed to excite their admiration; and, on their observing one of the seamen go aloft, their surprise exceeded all bounds. They gaped at him for a little time very silently, and then burst out into a most inordinate fit of laughter, which indeed appeared to be their general mode of expressing their surprise, for when any thing attracted their attention in a particular manner, they constantly broke out into shouts of laughter, or rather what may be deemed exclamations of surprise, as *hy ah! hy ah.*

After their astonishment had subsided a little, they began to show their predilection for different things : wood and iron in particular seemed to be what they most valued. They appeared to be of a thievish disposition; for one of them took up the armourer's sledge hammer, and having thrown it on the ice, immediately jumped after it, and picked it up : he then took to his heels, and, on finding himself pursued, threw it away, but did not return—a sufficient proof that he was aware of the impropriety of his conduct.

They were rather of a low stature, one of them, who was measured, being only five feet one inch and three-quarters high. Their features were rather broader than those of the natives we saw in Jacob's Bight, and to the southward. They all wore long beards, which were very thin ; but in almost every other respect resembled the Esquimaux already described. Their clothes were also of the same material, namely, seal-skins. Their frocks, or jackets, were indeed cut differently from those to the southward, they being provided with a flap before and behind, so as to resemble the jackets of the women in Jacob's Bight. Their breeches, if what they wore can be said to deserve that name, were also different from those we had seen before, for they came no higher than the upper part of the thigh, the rest being covered by the flaps of the jacket, which, when they stooped to pick up any thing, left their posteriors exposed.

They appeared to be altogether in a state of nature; and so perfectly ignorant were they of whatever belongs to every part of the globe, except that which they inhabit, that they considered the countries which lie to the southward, to be less fit for men to inhabit than their own, from the quantity of snow and ice, which they said they could never pass, always to be seen in that direction. They informed us, that their proper country lay to the northward of this, at a considerable distance, where there is but very little snow or ice, and, agreeably to Sacheuse's interpretation, *plenty of clear water,* that is, of sea. They said that they come hither in the summer season only, to hunt, and that in a little time they were to return to their own country, which they

represented as being governed by a king whose name was Too-
lowak, and the place of his residence Pitowak. How far these
stories are to be credited I am at a loss to say : we were not aware
however, of any motive these people could have in giving us
wrong information, and for that reason I think some degree of
credence may be bestowed on what they said, although it may be,
in certain respects, contrary to what we might have expected,
that is, with regard to the country to the northward being clearer
of snow and ice than where we now were. Some allowance is to
be made, at the same time, for Sacheuse's interpretation, as it
was with some difficulty that he made out what they said ; and
from his not being very well acquainted with the English language, it is probable that there may be a few errors in the narrative, as we received it from him. These people, as far as we
could learn, entertained very imperfect notions, if any, of a
supreme being.

It is plain that they have never been much to the southward of
this, for they never saw a ship before, nor even a canoe. From
this it is evident that they have not any communication with their
countrymen to the southward. It is certainly a remarkable circumstance, that people, inhabiting a sea coast, and who procure a
portion of what is essential to their existence from the ocean, as
is evidenced by their clothes being made of seals' skins, and their
spears of narwhals' horns, should be unprovided with canoes.
That such is the case, however, seems to be placed beyond a
doubt, not only by what we have learned from them, but by what
we have ourselves seen ; since nothing seemed to surprise them
more than a boat which was launched from the ice into the water ;
and, on being shown Sacheuse's canoe, they did not seem at all
to comprehend the use of it. This is a plain proof that navigation, even in its rudest state, is yet unknown to them ; for had they
ever ventured on the water, their vessels must have been made of
skins, as they have not any wood. Among other proofs, if such
were wanting, of their never having seen Europeans before, was
the astonishment they expressed at our clothes : after feeling
them, and smoothing them down for some time, they asked Sacheuse to what kind of a beast it was that these skins belonged,
not doubting but that, like their own, they were made of the skin
of some animal. Some other anecdotes, indicative of their utter
ignorance of what regards civilization, might be adduced : one of
them having been presented with a wine glass, appeared to be
very much astonished that it did not melt with the heat of his
hand, no doubt from an idea he entertained, at the first view, that
it was made of ice. A looking glass seemed to surprise them
equally, when they perceived their image reflected in it.

Their sledges were made entirely of bone, apparently of whale-bone   Each of the natives was provided with a kind of knife, made of small pieces, or plates of iron, which were set close together in a groove made in a piece of narwhal's horn : the end piece was rivetted, but the others were kept in their places merely by being driven tightly into the groove.   Very diligent enquiry was set on foot as to where they found the iron of which these knives were made ; but all we could learn from them was, that they met with it near the shore, at some distance from this place.   Our conjecture was, that it was native iron, and that they were afraid of giving us much information respecting it, from an apprehension of our taking it away.   They promised, however, to pay us another visit on the following day, and bring some of the iron with them.   I shall therefore forbear saying any thing further about them at present, as we shall probably learn a little more of them in the course of their second visit.

The ice having opened a little on the morning of Tuesday, the 11th, we cast off, and stood to the westward, along the edge of the land-floe.   I was apprehensive at the time, that we should not see any more of our late visitors ; but we had not gone far, before we were again stopped by the ice.   This renders it probable that we shall have another visit from them before we leave this place ; for, from the manner in which they were treated, and the presents they received, they will no doubt be as anxious to meet us again, as we shall be to see them.   These presents consisted of a few nails, a hammer, and a few pieces of wood, together with some other trifling articles, but could hardly be deemed presents, as the natives gave us some of their spears, made of the horns of the narwhal (monodon monoceros) in exchange for what they received.   They would probably have been on board of us to-day, had they not seen the ships get under weigh.

During the greater part of the following day, the 12th, it blew pretty fresh, and snowed with little intermission ; but as the wind was chiefly from the southward, (by compass : variation 92° 18′) it had but little effect in clearing away the ice in the direction in which we wished to proceed.   We were fast all the day to the edge of the land ice, under the lee of an iceberg, from which a large piece of ice fell, on the afternoon of yesterday, and crushed into thousands of fragments a considerable portion of a floe which was near to it, raising such a sea all around it as to be sensibly felt on board our ship, although we were, as nearly as I can judge, about three hundred yards from it.   Had we not been aware before of the danger of getting too near the perpendicular side of these bergs, this would have been an excellent lesson to us ; but we have seen of late so many instances of the same kind, that we are very cautious how we approach them.

On Thursday the 18th, in the morning, we got under weigh again, and ran a few miles to the westward, along the edge of the land floe, until we were, as usual, stopped by the ice, to which we again made fast. As there was not an immediate prospect of getting any further for some time, a pole, with a white flag on it, was stuck in the ice, at a considerable distance from the ships. Whether this pole, or the ships themselves, attracted the notice of the natives, I cannot say, but two of them drove out to it in their sledges, drawn in the customary manner, by dogs. They were no sooner observed than Sacheuse was dispatched to meet them; and on this occasion both parties advanced towards each other with greater boldness than on the preceding one, or, to speak more properly, Sacheuse advanced towards them with less hesitation, for they had already reached the pole on which the flag was flying, and remained there until he came to them.

After having conversed together for a short time, they were prevailed on to come on board. Little persuasion was indeed necessary on this occasion, as they had heard of the kind reception our first visitors met with, they having reported us to be very good people. Those to day did not appear to be either so much amazed at what they saw, or yet so timid, or rather suspicious, as the first party, which arose, no doubt, from their being more confident of their personal safety; a confidence founded on the reports of those who had preceded them. They evinced the same avidity for wood and iron as the former; and, in order to gratify them, they were presented with a few pieces of each. They likewise received some other useful articles, such as needles, scissars, &c., in return for which they gave narwhals' horns, one of their sledges, and a dog. They had knives similar to those already described; and it appears from what Sacheuse could gather from them, that they procure the iron of which they are made, from a mass of native iron, distant, agreeably to their information, about a day's journey to the eastward of this place. They likewise told him that their only object, in coming so far from their own country, which lies to the northward, is to procure some of this iron, which they break off with great difficulty by the means of stones, and then beat out into the small plates of which the knives are made. Thus far their description agrees so well with what we find these rude instruments to be, that I think there cannot be any doubt of the truth of what they have related.

On being afterwards more closely questioned respecting this iron, they said that there were two insulated masses of it, the largest of which they described as being about the size of the sky-light over Captain Ross's cabin, which is about four feet across. The other mass was reported by them to be considerably smaller.

The place where these masses lie, is called by them Soowilik, from Soowik, the name of iron in the Esquimaux language.

They entertained a singular notion respecting the place we are come from : it is no other than that we are from the moon. The reason they assigned for this whimsical idea is, that we are provided with so much wood, which, as they suppose, grows very abundantly there.

They had several other ridiculous notions respecting our ships. On our first appearance, they fancied each of the masts to be a tall man come to destroy them ; and so strongly were they impressed with the idea that the ships were animated beings, that one of the first questions they asked Sacheuse was, whether they could fly as well as swim ?

The ice being still close to the westward, we were necessarily obliged to pass the whole of the day of Friday, the 11th, in the same place, since the idea of pushing out among the loose or drifting floes to the southward, was, it would appear, considered to be highly dangerous, after what we had latterly experienced from leaving the land ice. The weather for the last two days had been in general thick, with occasional falls of snow, and a fresh breeze from the southward.

We had to-day another visit from the natives, whose number was greater than on the former occasions, there being nine in the party. They came, as usual, in their sledges, which they left, together with the dogs, on the ice, at the distance of about a mile from the ships. Notwithstanding these poor animals remained at this distance without any one to watch them, still they never stirred from the spot ; a strong proof, if any such proof were needed, of the sagacity of these faithful companions, or to express myself more properly, of these useful servants of man, in this remote part of the world. The number of them in each sledge varies, it being probably proportioned to the affluence of the owner, but is generally speaking, from five to seven. They are usually yoked in pairs, with a leader, or single one before. They are guided by the means of reins or thongs made of the skin of the walrus : or what appeared at least to us to be such from their thickness. On each sledge was an inflated seal skin, the use of which I apprehend to be to buoy up themselves and the sledge, when crossing the water which occasionally intervenes by the separation of the floes on which they may happen to be. Such a contrivance must be at times absolutely necessary to them, as they are unprovided with canoes ; for it is not unusual, whenever a change of wind happens, to find the ice separate in places, where there had not, until then, been the least appearance of such a division.

Their dread of these openings was evinced by the natives to

day in an extraordinary manner. After we had given them a few pieces of wood and iron, together with some other articles, and had obtained from them all the information they could supply, they were landed, or rather put on the ice : but, instead of going away, they collected alternately abreast of each ship, at the same time stretching out their hands towards us, and soliciting more wood and iron. At length their importunities became so tiresome, that we were obliged to have recourse to some means of getting rid of them ; and this was fully effected by the following expedient, which at once shows their super-stition, and their dread of the ice separating. One of the Isabella's men, having provided himself with a ship's trumpet, gave several loud blasts while they were abreast of her : they gazed at him for some time with apparent surprise ; but, on being told by Sacheuse that the trumpeter was an augekok who would not fail to blow away, in a little time, all the ice between them and the shore, if they did not depart very quickly, their surprise was suddenly converted into fear. This had the desired effect, as they betook themselves to their sledges without any farther delay.

Having, in the above passage, introduced the word *augekok*, which is not likely to be generally understood, it may be necessary to enter into a short explanation of its meaning. It implies a sorcerer, or diviner, who pretends to work miracles, to prophesy, and to hold converse with spirits. These people, who are the sages of the Greenlanders, from the power and wisdom they are supposed to possess, make themselves both feared and respected. They are consulted on every great occasion ; and, among other things, pretend to cure all diseases by amulets and magic spells. A long account of their impostures is given in Crantz's history of Greenland.*

Belonging to the party which came on board to day, was one who, according to Sacheuse, could speak like an augekok, although he did not pretend to be one of that fraternity. Our interpreter appeared to take great delight in hearing him converse with the devil, as he called it : this consisted of a low muttering quite contrary to the usual mode of speaking of the natives, which is very loud, as if conversing with a person at a distance. This Esquimaux also showed us the manner in which the seals are caught on the ice, which is done by lying down and grunting exactly like those animals, hopping along at the same time on the elbows, with a motion so perfectly resembling that of a seal, that it is by no means a matter of surprise that these stupid creatures should be deceived by it. He also gave us a song, which, however beautiful the composition may have been, had

---

* Vol. 1. p. 208, et seq.

certainly very little melody in it. At the end of every verse, or, at least, every now and then, his companions joined chorus. During the time he was singing, his body was in a constant motion, certainly not of the most decent kind, according to our ideas, but considered, perhaps, by them, to be very graceful.

Among these natives were some of those who had paid us the first visit, the one who had attempted to steal the sledge hammer being of the party. Another endeavoured to day to make off with a spy-glass, and a pair of razors, belonging to Captain Ross, thus plainly evincing their propensity to theft. With respect to their persons little is to be said, in addition to what has been already noticed. I have observed, as I had occasion to remark before, in describing the natives to the southward, that their feet and hands are exceedingly small, in proportion to the rest of the body. One of those on board had one leg shorter than the other : he was the only Esquimaux we had yet seen with any deformity.

These natives were, as usual, provided with narhawls'-horns, which they disposed of for their favourite articles, wood and iron. Some of their knives, similar to those already mentioned, were also procured by us : their average length was about ten inches, and the edge, instead of forming a straight line, was serrated at the parts where the different pieces of iron were joined, forming an edge somewhat resembling that of a serpentine Malay creesse.

On the following day, Saturday, the 15th, we had another visit from some of the natives, but they did not bring any thing with them beside two common stones. They were not allowed to come on board, because they had neglected to provide themselves with some of the iron they had promised yesterday. They went away shortly after apparently unsatisfied.

The number of rotges, on the water around the ship, has, if possible, increased within the last two days. As a proof of their great abundance, it will suffice to say, that, with three muskets, we killed this day, in the course of five or six hours, not less than one thousand, two hundred, and sixty-three, ninety-three of which were brought down by one discharge of the three muskets. A certain proportion of them has been regularly served out to the ship's company for some time past; and the others have been skinned, and packed up in casks between layers of pounded ice, which, it is imagined, will preserve them as long as may be needed in this country.

On the 16th, in the morning, a light breeze sprang up from the south-east. This, in the course of a few hours, drove the greater part of the loose ice off from the land floe, so that, in the afternoon, we got round the point, or promontory, to the westward, called by the natives Point Sichilik, which has for some time past bounded our view of the coast, as it has also been the

limit of our navigation. In consequence of our success to-day,
we feel as people always do after having surmounted a difficulty :
how long our prosperity is likely to continue we are unable to say ;
but there is certainly a much fairer prospect of our getting on
for some distance than we have had for some time past, the
coast being clear of ice as far as we can see. The ice is certainly
not far off it ; but if the wind should continue for any length of
time in the direction in which it is at present, it will, no doubt,
enlarge the space of clear water between the land and the ice,
and enable us to proceed. The land still trends to the westward
as far as we can see, the coast here is very bold, although not
particularly high : it is covered entirely with snow, with the
exception of the part facing the sea, which is so very steep that
the snow cannot rest upon it. In the vallies, however, it is
heaped up in large bodies. A considerable number of icebergs
lie off this coast ; but they are not so large as others we have
seen. This may be accounted for by the shallowness of the water
in this part, for, having sounded between three and four miles off
the shore, we found bottom in twenty-seven fathoms only.

After getting round the above-mentioned point or headland,
Sichilik, which is in latitude 75° 54′ 34″ north, and in longitude
66° 53′ 49″ west, it fell almost calm. The ships being close in
with the land an opportunity was afforded us of sending a boat
on shore. We landed on a low point close to the headland, and
found there the remains of several huts, which, from their
appearance could not have been inhabited for some years. Ad-
jacent to the ruins of these huts were several heaps, or rather
rude vaults, of loose stones, which were evidently burying places,
a human skull having been seen in one of them. The space
within which it was enclosed was between five and six feet long,
two feet broad, and about the same in height. On the face of the
hill, a little above the remains of the huts, we observed several
small piles of stones ; on examining two or three of them, we
found beneath them a number of rotges, there being in one of
them at least forty of these birds. They were without doubt
part of the store of the natives, probably of those who had for
some days past paid us visits, they having informed us that their
country lay to the northward, and that they were then merely on
a hunting excursion, if such a term can be applied to people wan-
dering about with no other arms than a narwhal's horn, and a
knife formed chiefly of the same material. The artifice displayed
yesterday, however, by the one who imitated the seal, makes it
probable that they are not without the means of procuring such
subsistence as their country affords.

How long the birds above mentioned had been killed, we could
not ascertain ; but probably not more than a month, as they ap-

peared to be in a good state of preservation, although they seemed not to have undergone any process for their preservation.
Their plumage was, as well as every other part, entire.   How the
natives contrived to kill them we could not conjecture; but this
was most likely done by throwing stones at them, for, on the face
of the hill near the spot where the above repositories were situated,
a great number of these birds were assembled on the rocks, and
seemed so regardless of our approach, that, had we been so inclined, we might have made great havoc among them in that way.
We remarked that near each store, or place where the birds were
deposited, several stones were set up on end, or two or three laid
one over the other; these we supposed to be intended for marks
to direct them to their respective collections, in the case of their
being covered by a fall of snow before their return.   They might
have been, however, marks by which each might know his own
particular store.

On the surface of the snow, close to where we landed, we met
with a description of a red substance, apparently of a vegetable
nature.   Something of the same kind is described* as having been
found on the surface of the snow, on the Alps and Pyrenees.
We brought some of it on board, as well as other specimens belonging to the vegetable and mineral kingdoms.   This substance,
whatever it may be, is very plentiful on this part of the coast, the
snow being covered with it, in different places, to a considerable
extent.   It is soluble in water, to which it gives a deep red colour;
but, when allowed to settle a little, sinks to the bottom, leaving the
water almost colourless.   It is worthy of remark that this colouring matter, be it what it may, does not penetrate more than an
inch or two beneath the surface of the snow; and, had it not
been that a similar substance appears to have been observed on
the snow, on the Alps and Pyrenees, where there could not be
any of the rotges, which are so numerous here, I should have
been inclined to think that the red, or colouring matter, alluded
to, is the excrement of these birds.   What renders this conjecture probable is, that we found great numbers of them seated on
the rocks, precisely over where the red snow lay.   I have already
observed that their food consists of small red shrimps.

On the point on which we landed, we found, contrary to our
expectations, several spots of thick coarse grass, in some places
eight or nine inches in length.   The soil was a description of soft
spungy moss, in some parts from two to three inches in thickness.
Such portions of it as were not covered with grass, presented a
beautiful surface of soft tufted moss, which the natives use as

---

* Rees's Encyclopedia.   Article Snow.

wicks to their lamps. We brought a considerable quantity on board with us.

Since we came round Point Sichilik, we have seen very few rotges on the water, and only one whale, which was close in with the shore as we landed this evening.

We made very little progress on the following day, the 17th, owing to the lightness of the wind. In the afternoon we were obliged to make fast to an iceberg, to avoid being carried away by the tide, which we found to be setting S. W., at the rate of one mile an hour. During the time we were fast to the berg, which was from two to four o'clock, the tide ebbed about twenty inches. If it be a regular tide of six hours, we may infer from this circumstance that it rises and falls about five feet.

An order was received to day from Captain Ross, respecting the manner in which any objects of Natural History which may happen to fall in our way, are to be disposed of in future. A copy of this order will be found in the Appendix, No. IV.

On the morning of Tuesday, the 18th, about nine o'clock, we were abreast of a small rocky island, which lay about three miles off a headland. To the westward of this the land trends N. E. by N., (by compass: variation 76° 56'.) Beyond this cape, we observed a remarkable difference in the appearance of the land. In the first place, it is much clearer of snow than any part of the coast we have yet seen, and, in the second place, is much lower than any land we have hitherto fallen in with in this country. It is besides quite differently shaped, its surface being more regular and even, and rising gradually from the sea side, where it is very low, towards the interior of the country. In a valley, a few miles to the westward of the above cape, or headland, an immense glacier extended from a considerable distance inland to the coast, and had, indeed, the appearance of stretching out for some way into the sea.

Off this part of the coast, we found, by the pitching motion both of the ships and icebergs, a considerable swell. The sea was still pretty clear of ice, and we were favoured by a fine breeze of wind during the whole of the day. In the afternoon we passed a large sound, with an island at its entrance, from which circumstance, connected with its distance from the headland, and the small island we passed in the morning, being, as nearly as we could estimate, twelve leagues, we have every reason to suppose the headland to be the Cape Dudley Digges of Baffin, and the sound, that which he named Sir John Wolstenholm's Sound. It would, indeed, be impossible, within the same compass of words, to give a more correct description of these places than the one contained in his journal;* but he must have been egregiously out in his latitude

---

* See Appendix, No. 3.

of Cape Dudley Digges, for we find the latitude of the headland we passed this morning to be 76° 05′ 24″ N. and its longitude 68° 16′ 50″ W. while he places the same, viz. Cape Dudley Digges, in latitude 76° 35′ N. Of the geographical position of Wolsten-holm's Sound he does not make any mention in the above jour-nal ; but we find, by the mean of several bearings, that the centre of Wolstenholm's Island, or, in other words, of the Island at the entrance of Wolstenholm's Sound, is in latitude 76° 29′ 39″ N., and in longitude 70° 40′ 46″ W. To the northward and westward of this island there is a remarkable piece of Table land, appa-rently an island ; and between this Table land and the Sound lies an insular conical rock, abreast of which we sounded this evening with a line of ninety fathoms, without finding bottom.

On Wednesday, the 19th, we came to a group consisting of seven or eight islands, three of which were considerably large : these we supposed to be Baffin's Carey islands. They lay, as nearly as we could estimate, off the coast, at about the distance he represents, namely, twelve or thirteen leagues. To the north-ward and eastward of them was a blank space, where not any land was discernible ; and this we supposed to be the entrance of Baffin's Whale Sound.* The centre of this opening bore N. 23° E. of us at noon (true bearings.) To the westward of this open-ing we could see the land a considerable distance very distinctly ; and about one o'clock it was reported that land was seen N. W., (by compass) and from that point all round to the mainland to the eastward. A report of such importance brought us all on deck immediately ; but for my own part, without trusting more to my imagination than to the evidence of my eyes, I could not venture to pronounce that I had seen any thing more than what is com-monly called the loom of the land. It was, indeed, said that a haze had come on soon after it was first seen : but it is to be hoped that all doubts on this subject will soon be decided by ocular de-monstration, to the entire satisfaction of every person who feels the least interested in the decision of so important a point. As far as I can judge, every thing at present (midnight) seems fa-vourable to this, as we have a fresh breeze from the southward and westward, (by compass) and the sea is quite clear of ice, with the exception of a loose stream to the north west. (by compass.)

Our latitude to day at noon was 76° 29′ 27″ N., and longitude 73° 14′ W. The variation, by the mean of several azimuths taken on board, was 101° 30′ W. The magnetic dip, as observed by Captain Sabine on an iceberg, was 85° 44′ 38″. The Carey islands bore at noon from N. 9° W. to N. 22° E. of us, (true)

---

* The latitude of *true* Cape Dudley Digges is about three miles farther from that given by Baffin, than the latitude of the Cape we mistook for it.

and the north-westernmost one of them was estimated to be about 12 miles distant from us, which would make its latitude to be about 76° 41' 21" N. and its longitude 73° 22' 30" W. At four P.M. we tried for soundings with a line of two hundred fathoms, without finding bottom. At seven o'clock in the evening the westernmost of the Carey islands bore N. 64° E. of us, (true) about nine or ten miles.

About ten o'clock the signal for Commander was made from the Isabella. Lieutenant Parry went on board, and received sealed orders from Captain Ross, to be opened in the event of parting company.

As the bearings and distances of the different places seen this day may be more readily understood by having them in the order in which they were taken, a copy of the ship's log, in which they are entered in that manner, is given in the Appendix, No. 5.

On Thursday, the 20th, at four in the afternoon, the weather having cleared up, we saw very distinctly the west land, said to have been seen yesterday, extending from N. ¼ E., to N. E. by E., (by compass) distant nine or ten leagues. The features of this land are quite different from those of the land we have lately passed, it being much more rugged, more elevated, and terminating in sharp cliffs, not unlike that to the southward of Ris-coll, or the land which we first saw after entering the Straits. It differs also from that lately seen, in being almost completely covered with snow. Shortly after the west land was seen, one of the Carey Islands was observed to bear S. by W. (by compass.)

During the remainder of the day, I passed the greater part of my time on deck, anxious to see whether the mainland to the eastward, that is, the coast of Greenland, and that to the westward, joined; but this I had not, at any time, the good fortune to see, although from ten o'clock until midnight the weather was remarkably fine and clear. It is probable that the chasm, or open space, to the northward, where not any land could be traced *by me*, might be that which Baffin calls Sir Thomas Smith's Sound; and if, agreeably to his relation, this is the " deepest and largest sound in all this bay," it is not likely that we should have seen the bottom of it at such a distance, as we estimate that we are twenty leagues from the northern extreme of the west land visible. By this estimation, the latitude of the northernmost land seen must be about 77° 39' N. which is twenty-one miles on this side, (to the southward) of where Baffin places the bottom of Sir Thomas Smith's Sound.

Our latitude, to day at noon, was 76° 40' 52" N., and at fifty minutes after twelve o'clock, P. M., being the time when we were farthest north, 76° 46' 40" N. Our longitude at that time, by account, was 73° 56' W. The magnetic dip was taken on an iceberg in the afternoon, and found, by the mean of three observ-ers, namely, Captain Sabine, Lieutenant Parry, and Mr. Bush-nan to be 86° 08′ 92″. They found also at this iceberg, a tide setting E. by N. (true), at the rate of one mile per hour : it was ebbing, but fell an inch or two only at the time they were there.

We found soundings at night in eighty-five fathoms. There was then a remarkable difference in the specific gravity of the sea water, it being 1027·1 (temperature 42°) which is greater than we had found it since the fifth day of July.

Between eleven and twelve o'clock, P. M. we made sail to the southward, and abandoned the search for a passage in this quarter, from a thorough conviction, I should hope, that not any such passage exists here. I am perfectly satisfied myself that this is not the place to look for it, although I must confess that I did not see the continuity of land all around the top of this bay, if it may be so termed ; and, in order to show that I am not the only person who has been unfortunate in this respect, I have in-serted, in the Appendix, No. 6, an exact copy of the ship's log for this day, by which it does not appear that the land was seen all around at one time ; neither, by a comparison of the bearings of the east land, and of the west, taken at different times, do they appear to meet.

On Friday, the 21st, on the west land, nearly opposite to where we were last night, before we made sail, we saw an im-mense glacier, which extended, from a large valley, at least two or three miles into the sea, and sloped gradually from the land towards its outer edge, which was, I think, full three miles in breadth. I do not entertain any doubt but that the icebergs are fragments of these glaciers, when they break off from the land.

During the whole of the last night and this morning, we were running to the southward, along the west coast, until we came to an opening between the west land, and another land, apparently an island, which lay off it. Here we met with a considerable quantity of loose ice, and, the weather becoming thick and hazy, made fast to an iceberg about half-past eleven o'clock in the forenoon. At eight A. M. when the last bearings of the land were taken, the southern extreme of the west land bore N. by W. and the land, apparently an island, to the southward of the inlet, which we suspected to be Baffin's Alderman Jones's Sound, N. W. by N.

We sounded alongside of the iceberg to which we were fast, in one hundred and thirty-five fathoms, mud and shells. On one side of it, where the sea washed into a little valley over the ice, we found an immense number of clias, and a species of medusa which we had not met with before; the small tentacula around its sides were in constant motion, and presented the most beau-tiful colours, chiefly of a purplish hue. We tried to preserve some of them in spirit, but they were no sooner thrown into it than they dissolved, or rather collapsed. We now begin to have a little darkness for about an hour towards midnight, insomuch that a candle is necessary to see to read or write below.

The weather during the whole of Saturday, the 22d, being foggy, we did not cast off from the iceberg. A pole, fifteen feet in height, with a piece of board nailed across the top of it, having these words cut on it—"Isabella, John Ross. Dig here," was planted on it, and underneath was buried a cylinder, containing some papers.

On Sunday the 23d, the weather having cleared up a little, with a light breeze from the W. S. W. (by compass: variation 107° W.) we cast off from the iceberg between eleven and twelve o'clock in the forenoon, and made sail to the southward among loose ice, which we found to be rather heavier, that is thicker, than any we had latterly met with. During the afternoon some parts of the western land were seen occasionally through the haze, but indistinctly.

On the following morning, at eight o'clock, there not being any wind, and the weather being thick and hazy, we made fast to a low iceberg. On different pieces of ice which we passed yesterday and this morning, we observed several tracks of bears, one of which was measured, and gave the following results.

	feet.	inches.
Length of the impression of the hind paw...	1	11
Breadth of ditto.....................................	1	1
Length of the impression of the fore-paw...	1	1
Breadth of ditto.....................................	1	0
Length of the fore-part of one footstep to the hind part of the fourth behind it.......	7	10

We traced this track to the edge of the ice, where the animal must have taken to the water, unless the floe was large, or in contact with other ice at the time he was on it.

In the afternoon we tried, by the self-registering thermometer, the temperature of the sea at different depths. At two hundred and forty fathoms it was 29½°; at a hundred fathoms, 30°; and at the surface, 31½°, the temperature of the air in the shade at the time being 33°.

For the last two days, seals have been seen in greater numbers than usual. Sixty two of them were counted on the ice at one time, by Mr. Beverley.

A piece of fir-wood, about eighteen inches in length, a good deal water-logged, but not worm eaten, was picked up by the Isabella to day. It had the mark of a saw near the middle, and another mark, either of a saw or axe, near the end. It had also a crooked nail in it, and the rust mark of another. The nail was rather of an unusual shape, being flat, and the head of it large in proportion to its size. As we are not aware that, since the time of Baffin, any ship has been so far north, in this part of the world, as where this piece of wood was picked up, we may conclude that it has floated hither from the southward, unless it be conceded that it has remained here since the time of the above navigator, which I think is scarcely possible.

On Tuesday, the 25th, in the morning, we cast off from the iceberg; but the wind was so light that the little progress we made was chiefly by the boats towing. About one o'clock P. M., we discharged three rifles at an immense Seal which lay on a piece of ice we passed. We suspected that he had been struck by the three balls from the quantity of blood he left on the ice : he managed, however, after some struggling, to get into the water before our boat reached him. He then came up once or twice to draw breath, and finally disappeared, as I understand is done by these animals when killed, or mortally wounded.

In the afternoon both ships again made fast to an iceberg, alongside of which we sounded in fifty-four and a half fathoms water, bottom small stones and shells. The highest part of this berg, above the surface of the water, was ninety-two and a half feet, and its diameter six hundred and three feet. From the former of these dimensions it would appear that the proportion of its height above, to that beneath the surface, differed from what we had hitherto found to be almost an invariable rule, namely, as one to seven. It ought, however, to be recollected, that the height of its most elevated part is the one given above, its general height having been estimated at about fifty feet, insomuch that the proportion of one to seven may still be considered to hold good. By trying in salt water a cube made from it, as on former occasions, we had indeed an evident proof that such is the case. The result of this experiment, and that of the other observations made to day, are as follow.

The sides of the cube measured forty-eight lines, seven of which were above the surface of the water, which, at the time of the experiment, was at the temperature of thirty degrees, and of the specific gravity of 1025·5.

	°	′	″
The observed latitude at noon was	76	08	28, N.
Longitude by chronometer	78	34	52 W.
Variation, by the mean of two Azimuths taken on the iceberg	109	35	58 W.
Magnetic dip, as taken by Captain Sabine on the iceberg	85	59	15

A cylinder was buried on the top of this berg also, with a

staff planted near it, having an inscription similar to the one
mentioned on the 22nd instant.

On the following day, the 26th, a little after six in the morning, we cast off from the iceberg, and made sail : but the wind
was so light, that our progress was very trifling. During the
greater part of the morning the weather was thick and hazy,
but cleared up a little about eleven o'clock, so that we had a
sight of some parts of the land. At this time a remarkable, high,
conical rock was seen off a headland bearing S. 40 W., four or
five leagues. At the entrance of the opening, or inlet, (query,
Alderman Jones's Sound) off which we have been for some days
past, we met with some of the largest icebergs we had yet seen :
several of them I should take to have been upwards of a mile in
length.

We passed several pieces of ice to day with large stones on
them. A boat having been lowered from each of the ships, for
the purpose of procuring a few specimens of these, those which
were brought on board the Alexander, were a species of grey granite,
broken off from a mass which must have weighed at least five or
six hundred weight. We saw on the ice a considerable number of
Seals. Ivory Gulls, (larus eburneus) and Kittiwakes, have also
been seen in greater numbers than usual ; but it is somewhat
remarkable that we have scarcely met with any rotges since we
passed Point Sichilik on the 10th instant. What is still more
unaccountable is, that we have not seen a single whale since that
time, unless we reckon the one we fell in with on the evening
when we went on shore on the west side of that headland. During
the afternoon we sounded several times, and found bottom in
sixty-three, sixty-eight, and seventy-five, fathoms, mud and
sand, sand and coral, and clear sand. We were surrounded by
loose ice and icebergs ; but the sea was so open that we could
not complain of much interruption.

The weather still continued thick on Thursday, the 27th,
with occasional showers of rain. We had a fresh breeze from
the S. W., (by compass) which enabled us to make some progress to the southward. Our latitude at noon, by account, was
75° 42′ 40″ N., and our longitude, 77° 56′ 30″ W. We sounded
about this time, and found bottom in ninety-five fathoms, sand
and small stones.

It was observed this day that the compasses traversed worse
than ever, at the same time that the deviation was much greater
than we had hitherto found it, insomuch that the ship's head,
on different tacks, lay within seven points of the compass :
for, by one of the Alexander's compasses, which are esteemed the
best, placed on the box fitted on the companion, her head on
one tack was W. N. W., and on the other, S. W. by S., the
wind remaining steady, as was evident from our observing this

after going about several times. It should be noticed that we were now passing the parallel of latitude where we found 90° of variation to the eastward, from which circumstance it is natural to suppose, that if we had had an opportunity at this time to observe the variation, we should have found it the same, but the magnetic dip much greater. This is on the supposition that the magnetic pole is situated in the parallel of latitude we crossed this day; and it certainly would have been very desirable to have had an opportunity of deciding this point by actual observation. In the evening we were in the midst of very heavy ice, and rather closer than we have had it for some time past, but the breeze being still pretty fresh, we managed to force our way through it.

The weather was still hazy on the 28th, so that we had but an indifferent observation at noon; our latitude by it was 75° 21′ N. In the afternoon we had an indistinct view of the land, which appeared to trend S. ½ W., true bearings. The tops of the hills were more rounded than those to the northward on this side; but our distance from the land was too great to enable us to say much respecting its appearance. In the course of the afternoon we were abreast of three remarkable hills, which were seen above the haze or fog by which the rest of the land was concealed at the time; they bore about west of us (true). In the evening we passed through a stream of heavy ice, which was the only ice we met with throughout the day. We had such a swell from the southward as led us to suppose that there was neither land nor much ice near us in that direction; and certainly clear water was more particularly desirable at this time, as we were beginning to lose light for two or three hours about midnight, we having been obliged this night, for the first time, to have a light in the binnacles, and in the gun-room.

During the forenoon of Saturday, the 29th, the weather was, as it had been in general for some time past, thick and foggy, to such a degree that we could not get a meridian altitude of the sun. Our latitude, by account, was 74° 58′ N., and longitude, also by account, 77° 42′ W. In the afternoon, however, the weather cleared up, so as to afford us a pretty good view of the land, the bearings of which were taken, and were as follow.

At 8 o'clock, P. M. extremes of the land from N. E. by E., to N. by E. ½ E., the land trending here S. E. by E., and N. W. by W. Another part of the land, high and rugged, W. N. W. by compass: the nearest part of the land distant six or seven leagues. About two hours before these bearings were taken, we sounded in one hundred and ninety-five fathoms, sand and small stones.

From the latitude we are now in, we have reason to suppose

that the opening, or inlet, between N. by E. $\frac{1}{2}$ E., and the land to the southward, bearing W. N. W. is the entrance of Baffin's Sir James Lancaster's Sound; and if we may venture to question the authority of that navigator, respecting his having seen the bottom of this inlet, or, as he calls it, I suspect gratuitously, sound,* it certainly has more the appearance of being the entrance of the wished-for straits, than any place we have yet seen. In the first place, the sea is perfectly clear of ice; and, secondly, the water is warmer than we have found it since the 7th instant, being 36° at the surface, and 31° at the bottom. The swell of the sea, the breadth of the opening, and the depth of the water, are all flattering appearances, independently of which we are not at a great distance from where the sea was seen by Mr. Hearne, at the mouth of the Coppermine river.

On the morning of Sunday, the 30th, the wind being from the eastward (by compass), we stood into the inlet above-mentioned, and the more we advanced, the more sanguine our hopes were that we had at last found what has been for ages sought in vain. Every thing, indeed, tended to confirm this our belief: at noon we tried for soundings with two hundred and thirty-five fathoms of line, without finding bottom; and in the evening, when the sun was getting low, the weather being remarkably clear, we could see the land on both sides of the inlet for a very great distance, but not any at the bottom of it. The bearings taken of the extremes of the land at this time are as follow.

" At 6 P. M. fresh breezes and cloudy weather. Northern land of the inlet from N. E. $\frac{1}{4}$ N. to E. by N. $\frac{3}{4}$ N.; cape bearing N. E. $\frac{1}{4}$ N. having a deep notch near the extremity. Southern land of the inlet from S. W. by W. $\frac{1}{2}$ W. Strong appearance of land S. E. by S."

" At 8, moderate breezes and fine weather, with a swell from N. W.: tacked. Southern land extending from S. W. by W. $\frac{1}{4}$ W. to N. W. $\frac{1}{2}$ W. The nearest part of it N. W. by W distant nine or ten miles. The whole of this land high, with many pointed hills, much covered with snow, and several large glaciers on it; this part of the coast appearing to trend about N. $\frac{1}{2}$ E. and S. $\frac{1}{2}$ W. the northern land, beginning with the Cape before-mentioned as having a remarkable notch in it, N. 44° E. to E. by N. $\frac{1}{2}$ N. perceived the deviation of the compasses to be one point from one tack to the other."

Alexander's log.

---

* Indeed, although he calls it a sound, his own words do not imply that he saw the bottom of it. They are as follow. "On the 12th day we were open of another sound, lying in the latitude of 74° 20′ N., and we called it Sir James Lancaster's sound. Here our hopes of a passage began to be less, &c."

The land on the south side of the inlet was high, and full of sharp-pointed hills, which were completely covered with snow, having an appearance unusually grand. In the vallies there were several large glaciers. The coast appeared to trend W. by S. (true.) The land on the north side did not appear to be either so high or so rugged as that on the opposite side, its western visible extremity being bounded by a cape, or headland, with a notch in it. This headland bore about N. 62 W. (true.) The other extreme of this land bore about N. 32 W. (true.)

The breadth of the inlet was estimated to be from ten to twelve leagues. Our latitude, to day at noon, was 74° 21' 08" N. and longitude, by chronometer, 79° 01' 46" W. At night we saw several stars, for the first time since we crossed the Arctic circle. Although we hailed them at first as old friends, bringing into recollection the happy change of day and night in our native clime, still on a little reflection, we could not fail to consider them as the harbingers of that dreary season which must, in a little time, suspend our researches in these regions, unless we should be so fortunate as to accomplish the object in view before that period arrives.

The wind having been rather against us (N. N. W. by compass) during the whole of the night, we made but little progress; but on the following morning, the 31st, every thing tended, if possible, to increase our hopes. Not any ice was to be seen in any direction; and at seven o'clock, the weather being remarkably fine and clear, land was not to be discerned between N. 21° W., and N. 44° E. At this time our distance from the northern land was estimated at seven or eight leagues, and from the southern, six or seven leagues; but, alas! the sanguine hopes and high expectations excited by this promising appearance of things were but of a short duration, for, about three o'clock in the afternoon, the Isabella tacked, very much to our surprise indeed, as we could not see any thing like land at the bottom of the inlet, nor was the weather well calculated at the time for seeing any object at a great distance, it being somewhat hazy. When she tacked, the Isabella was about three or four miles ahead of us, so that, considering the state of the weather, and a part of this additional distance, for we did not tack immediately on her tacking, but stood on towards her, some allowance is to be made for our not seeing the land all around. Ocular demonstration would certainly have been very satisfactory to us, on a point in which we were so much interested; but we must be content, as there cannot be any doubt but that all in the Isabella were fully convinced of the continuity of land at the bottom of this inlet, or, as I may now venture to call it, agreeably to Baffin, sound. In order to show the vacant space, or opening, where we did not see any land, a correct copy of the ship's log for this day is inserted in the Appendix, No 7. In this the different bearings, as well as the other nautical remarks, are noted in the order in which they were taken. Our latitude at noon, by account, was 74° 08′ 56″ N. and longitude, by chronometer, 80° 29′ 55″ W. At the time we tacked, namely, at forty minutes past three P. M., our latitude, by account, was 74° 14′ 50″, and our longitude, also by account, 81° 09′ 50″ W. This was our farthest progress west in the inlet, or sound.

During the whole of the night we were running out of the inlet; and in the morning of September 1st, were so clear of it, that the northern land was but very indistinctly seen. The sea was perfectly clear of ice, with a considerable swell, and the weather remarkably fine and clear. We continued running along the coast, which trends about N.N. W. and S.W. by S. (by compass: variation 108) until one o'clock, P. M., when the Isabella hove to abreast of an open bay, and between six and seven miles from the shore. Here she sounded in one thousand fathoms, soft muddy bottom; and, when within three miles of the shore, in not less than seven hundred fathoms. The object of heaving to here was said to be that of taking possession of this part of the coast. The Isabella sent two boats on shore, one of them provided with a pole similar to those which had been planted on the icebergs: this was erected on the top of a round hill, on the south side of the bay.

The signal was made for two of the Alexander's boats also to be sent on shore: we landed on a fine sandy beach, on which the sea broke with considerable violence. There appeared to be at least eight or nine feet rise and fall of tide here; for during the time we were on shore, that is, from half-past two to half-past five, the tide ebbed, as nearly as we could estimate, about four feet and a half. If we were to judge, however, of the rise and fall of the tide, from the distance from the water at which we found several whales' bones, it might be conjectured to be at least twelve or fourteen feet.

It was supposed that the time of high-water to-day was between twelve and one o'clock, the moon being two days old. The whales' bones having been found so high up on the beach is not to be regarded as a sufficient proof that the tide rises so high as where they lay. It is most probable that they were thrown up there by the surf, which, when the wind blows hard into the bay, must undoubtedly run high; for this day even, although there was little, if any wind, a considerable surf broke on the beach. Independently of this, the bones in question might have been dragged beyond the tide mark by bears.

Six of those particular bones called the "crown bone," lay within a short distance of each other, besides several other bones, which, from their size, left no doubt of their having belonged to the same animal, or rather fish. Some of the vertebræ were of an enormous magnitude. I did not measure them, but I may venture to say that several were at least eighteen or twenty inches in diameter.

Near the centre of the valley where we landed, we came to a considerable stream of fresh water: from the size of the bed or channel in which it flowed, it may be concluded that the quantity of water which ran here at times was much greater than at present. The breadth of this channel was estimated to be about fifty yards, and its depth upwards of twenty feet. We walked along the right bank for some distance, and there picked up a great variety of mineral and vegetable productions, some of them quite different from any we had seen before. Several pieces of flint were picked up: and limestone appeared to be very plentiful. Some of the latter having been burned, was found, on being slaked, to afford excellent lime. In several of the pieces we found small portions of flint embedded, and in one of them in particular the flint passed through like a kind of vein.

It would require an able botanist to describe the different vegetable productions we met with : some of them were extremely beautiful, but they were all of a dwarfish size, not any of them being larger than the creeping or ground willow, which seldom or ever exceeds the thickness of a man's finger. This sterility must certainly be owing to the rigour of the winter, as there was a considerable layer of soil along the banks of the above stream. Throughout the whole of the valley, which was of considerable extent, not a particle of snow was to be seen. The tops of the hills were, indeed, covered with it, but their sides, for a considerable distance up, were as clear of it as the sea shore.

We were very much surprised at not finding any inhabitants in this place, which is, according to our ideas, the fittest for man to live in of any we have seen since we came to these regions. It appeared indeed to be but thinly inhabited by any of the animal creation. A white bear was seen by those who landed first : on being fired at, it plunged into the sea, and escaped. Our party killed a white hare, a pine martin, and one or two snipes ; but I had not the good fortune myself to see one living creature, with the exception, on our first land-ing, of two or three of the birds just mentioned. We met with the track of some cloven-footed animal, probably, a rein-deer : it was recent, and being on moist sand, an opportunity was afforded us of ascertaining its dimensions very correctly. They are as follow,

	Ft.	In.
Length of the hoof...	0	7½
Breadth of ditto..	0	5½
From the fore part of one footstep to the fore part of the fourth behind it..	9	0

This agrees pretty nearly with the tracks measured on the even-ing of the 21st of June, but mentioned among the occurrences of the day following.

The most curious object, however, met with by us, although in itself not of any value, was a piece of birch bark which I picked up in a small brook at least half a mile from the beach. How it came there is certainly a subject of interesting inquiry, since we did not see any wood growing, nor did we perceive any traces of human beings, to lead us to suppose that it had been brought thither by them. Is it possible that it had been carried from the southward by the water which flows down this valley ? It was not found in the channel described above, so that, had it been carried down by the stream which runs there, the latter must at the time have overflowed its banks, for the place where it was picked up was at least three hundred yards from it. This was, as well as all the other specimens, both mineral and vegetable, sent to Captain Ross, agreeably to the order issued on the 17th of the last month. Among other substances which we considered curious, was a kind of black coarse-grained stone, which, on being broken, emitted a smell somewhat similar to that of a mixture of different drugs.

An azimuth and sights for chronometers were taken at the place at which we landed, and the results are as follow.

	°	′	″
Latitude of the place of observation, by account	73	30	00 N.
Longitude, by chronometer (509).....................,	77	24	09 W.
Variation, by azimuth (indifferent)...................	109	32	53 W.

In the evening we saw several large fish, having on the back a long fin, which was seen every now and then a considerable height above the surface of the water. They were supposed to be whales of the species called by the fishermen " bottle noses."

From the time we left the above-mentioned bay, up to Sun-day, the 6th, nothing occurred worthy of notice. We kept running along the coast, which trended about N. E. and S. W. (by compass,) but at such a distance from it, that, owing to the haziness of the weather, we had but occasional glimpses of it.

Little respecting it can therefore be said: it seemed to be in general high, and covered with snow. Where we were, on the above day, there appeared to be a tide or current setting to the southward, for at noon our latitude by observation was thirteen miles to the southward of that given by account, the former being 72° 22′ N., and the latter 72° 35′ N. In the afternoon we sounded in four hundred and three fathoms, brown, muddy bottom: the self-registering thermometer was attached to the lead in sounding; but the mercury having got above one of the indices, not any reliance could be placed in the temperature shown by it, which was 30, the water at the surface being at the time 37°. The sea was, as it had indeed been since the 29th of the last month, perfectly clear of ice: we occasionally saw a few icebergs, but not any thing to interrupt us.

The two following days were as barren of events as the preceding week. The land was seen on the 7th at a considerable distance, but not on the day succeeding: in the forenoon, however, something like the loom of it was perceived. If we should continue the course we have been steering during the afternoon of this latter day (the 8th) it is probable that the coast of Greenland will be the first land we shall see, unless such a place as James Island exists, of which I believe there are some doubts.

During the forenoon of Wednesday, the 9th, we altered our course, and steered more to the westward. At four o'clock P. M., the weather having cleared up, we saw land bear N. W. ½ W. of us ; it differed in appearance from that which we had lately passed, for along the coast, and for a considerable distance inland, it was low and level. Beyond, there were several round-topped hills, which we mistook at first, that is, before we approached the coast, for islands. Between seven and eight o'clock in the evening we sounded in forty-five fathoms, muddy bottom. We were then about seven or eight miles from the nearest part of the coast, which bore as follows.

A bold cape N. 3° E., from which the land was seen extending as far as N. 9° W. Not any land was then discernible until a point bearing N. 15° W., from which land was seen as far as N. 80° W., where there was a remarkable pointed hill. From this the land extended as far as S. 52° W., its trending appearing to be N. E. and S. W. by compass : variation 104.)

What this land is, it is impossible, I think, to say ; but it is probably that laid down in the charts under the name of Cumberland Island. In the afternoon we passed a few icebergs and pieces of loose ice ; and a whale was seen for the first time since we passed Cape Sichilik, unless, as I have already remarked, that which we saw the night we doubled that headland be reckoned to the westward of it. It would indeed appear, from what we have seen, that whales are seldom to be met with among the ice.

During the whole of the 10th, we coasted along the land, which was still low near the sea, but rose inland to a considerable height. It was there rugged, and, as usual, covered with snow : every part of this land was indeed covered with it ; but that on the low land was very thin, and, to all appearance, had lately fallen.

About ten o'clock in the morning, a large white bear was observed swimming towards the ship from the shore ; and a boat was immediately lowered to go after him. On finding himself pursued, he made every attempt to get away, both by swimming and diving.* After he had received two rifle balls, we ran our boat alongside of him ; but even then he made a furious defence, by laying hold, with his mouth and fore paws, of the pikes and whale lances with which we assailed him. The contest, however, was not long ; for in a few minutes he was overpowered with the number and severity of his wounds, and, what was very mortifying to us, sunk just as we were in the act of throwing the bight of a rope round his neck, in order to secure him. We were not less surprised than disappointed, no one in the boat having the most distant idea that he would sink. It was not long, however, before we had an opportunity of availing ourselves of the experience we had gained, for between twelve and one o'clock, P. M. another bear, of the same description, was seen swimming close to the ship. Two boats were immediately dispatched after him : we fired two balls at this one also, before we closed with him, but they had so little effect, that he made a still more desperate defence than the former. He bit the head, or iron part, of one of the boarding-pikes clean off in the middle, and, when he found it impossible to escape, roared in the most hideous manner, at the same time warding off some of the thrusts which were made at him, by the means of his fore paws, and likewise attempting to get into each of the boats,† on the bows of which he left evident marks of his claws and teeth. In conformity to the order issued on the 17th ultimo, respecting

---

* This does not, however, constitute an amphibious animal.

† This leads me to mention an accident which occurred this summer to Mr. Hawkins, master of the Everthorpe, of Hull, who nearly lost his life in an attack on a bear. The animal laid hold of him by the thigh, dragged him out of the boat, and swam away with him to some distance, before he let him go. He would, without a doubt, have destroyed him, had he not been pursued by the boat.

objects of natural history, he was no sooner secured, than we towed him alongside the Isabella, from which I have collected the following particulars of measurements, &c. and brought them into comparison with those of the bear killed by Captain Phipps.

A comparison of the different measurements of the bear killed by Captain Phipps, in his voyage to Spitzbergen, and of the one killed by the crews of the boats of his Majesty's ship Alexander, in Davis' Straits.

	Phipps.		Alexander.	
	feet.	inches.	feet.	inches.
Length from snout to tail..........	7	1	7	8
Ditto, to shoulder blade............	2	2	2	10
Height of the shoulder............	4	3		
Circumference near the fore legs.	7	0	6	0
Ditto, of the neck....................	2	1	3	2
Breadth of the fore paw............	0	7	0	10
Ditto of the hind paw....................			0	8½
Circumference of the hind leg....................			1	10
Ditto, of the fore leg....................			1	8
Ditto, of the snout, before the eyes....................			1	10
Length of the head, from the tip of the snout to the occiput....................			1	3
Length of the fore claws............................. .			0	2½
Ditto, of the hind claws....................			0	1½
Ditto, of the tail....................			0	5
Weight, exclusive of that of the blood he lost, estimated at nineteen pounds........................			1131 lbs.	

The polar bear may almost be classed among the amphibious animals, being not only an excellent swimmer, but an expert diver, as we had a very good opportunity of witnessing to day. Their venturing so far from the land as where we found them on this occasion, is, besides, a very strong proof how much these animals trust to their swimming. The one we killed in the forenoon, was, I think, at least six miles from the shore, and there was not any ice near, on which he could rest himself. The one killed in the afternoon was about the same distance from the mainland ; but nearly half way between our ships and the coast, there was a small island.

To this island the Isabella sent a boat, for the purpose of erecting on it a staff similar to the one planted on the top of a hill on the 1st instant. Those who landed did not meet with any inhabitants ; but there were evident marks of the island having been lately visited, for they came to a spot where a fire had been kindled, around which were several bones, probably those of a seal, which appeared to be fresh, or, in other words, to have belonged to an animal recently killed : they likewise found a human skull. It was Sacheuse's opinion, that these visitors were without canoes ; and his principal reason for supposing this was, that there were numerous tracks of dogs in the vicinity. If he was right in his conjecture, they must have left the island before the ice between it and the mainland was broken up.

On the morning of Friday, the 11th, the weather being fine, and there being but little wind, Lieutenant Parry asked permission to measure an iceberg at a small distance from us : as it appeared to be longer than any we had yet seen in these regions, we were anxious to ascertain its size. The request was granted ; but our object was nearly frustrated, by the inaccessible form of the berg. One of the Isabella's boats, which happened to be a short distance before us, went into a little creek, on one side of it, which appeared to be the only place where it was possible to get upon it, on the side we first made. On examining this place, however, they considered it too difficult for the attempt ; so that, without any further examination, the boats pulled right round the berg. This was a labour of some hours ; and, what was still more grievous, there was not a single place where we could possibly attempt to get up, the sides of the iceberg being as perpendicular as the walls of a house, and between forty and fifty feet high, at an average. After performing a circuit round this enormous mass of ice, we returned again to the above-mentioned creek, where, after some difficulty, one of our men scrambled up : by the means of a line which he made fast to the top, we all got up, and that without much loss of time, for the man who first ascended, on looking round, observed a white bear at a little distance from him. We prepared ourselves immediately to attack this formidable animal, some with muskets, and the others with lances and boarding pikes. He at first advanced towards us ; but on perceiving that our approaches were mutual, took to his heels towards the opposite side of the berg. As we were, however, acquainted with its height, as well on that, as on every other side, we made ourselves quite sure of securing him ; and, in order to be more expeditious, divided ourselves into two parties, for the purpose of hemming him in : but, very much to our disappointment, and contrary to our expectations, we found that he had leaped off the berg, at a place where we estimated its height to be about fifty feet. On looking over the precipice at this part, I observed several large fragments of ice floating at the bottom, on one of which he is supposed to have fallen, and to have been killed, as we did not see him afterwards. He was not so large as either of those we killed the day before; but we found the tracks of several large ones on the berg. The entrance by which we supposed they got on it was through a kind of vault, or cavern, which led from the creek where we left the boats, to a small valley into which the sea flowed. After our fruitless chase of the bear, we proceeded to measure the iceberg, the dimensions of which, and the result of the observations made on it, are as follow.

Size, weight, and solid contents of an iceberg measured on the 11th of September, 1818, in Davis' Straits, latitude 70° 36′ 40″N., and longitude 67° 27′. 45″ W. Its length and breadth were obtained by actual measurement, and its thickness by comparing its actual height above the surface of the sea with the portion of a cube* made from it above the surface of the sea water, when floating in it. Its weight was estimated by weighing a cube made from it, a solid inch having been found to weigh two hundred and forty grains.

	miles.	yards.	feet.	inches.
Length..............................	2 and 649 or 12·507			0

Breadth, three thousand eight hundred and sixty-nine paces, estimating each pace at two feet, nine inches...............

	miles.	yds.	ft.	inches.	ft.	inches.
	2 and 26	1	9 or 10·639 and 9			

Thickness, allowing fifty-one feet to be the average height above the surface of the sea, as was found to be the height of the place where it was measured.

	feet.	inches.	lines.
	367	2	4

Solid contents in feet   48·863·800·913 and 691½ inches.
Ditto in inches......   84·436·647·978·355½ inches.
Weight in tons......   1·292·397·673· 2cwt. 3qrs. 1lb. 5oz. 2dw. 5$\frac{8}{10}$grs.

N.B. The weight and dimensions of this iceberg, as given above, are to be considered only as an approximation to the truth.

Variation on the iceberg, by azimuth, 77° W.

For the sake of amusement, it was calculated what space the quantity of ice in this iceberg would cover, if reduced to the thickness of six inches, which it was presumed would

---

* The sides of the cube measured thirty-six lines, and in salt water, at the temperature of 35°, and of the specific gravity of 1024·9, five lines of it were above the surface of the water. The specific gravity of the water obtained by dissolving this cube was 1000·6, the temperature of the water at the time of the experiment, being 51°.

be sufficiently strong for the purpose of skaiting. From the result of this calculation it would appear to be sufficient to cover a space equal to 3,505 square miles, 31 square furlongs.

On the afternoon of Sunday, the 13th, we passed an iceberg with a large white bear on it. This tends, in some measure to confirm what I remarked a few days ago, respecting the amphibious nature of these animals. It was understood on board that, at the time we passed him, we were about the middle of the Straits. Be this as it may, it is certain that he must have been at a great distance from the land, it not having been seen by us for these two days past. What is still more extraordinary, I have been informed by those of the seamen who have been in this country before, that they have met with bears swimming where neither land nor ice was to be seen.

While passing through a stream of ice, on Tuesday, the 15th, we observed two large bears lying on two small portions of it. The spray of the sea occasionally went over them; but this they appeared not to notice. They were not so far from the land as the one seen on Sunday last, the west coast being in sight at the time. Several flocks of wild ducks were also seen on this day, together with some land birds, one of which was caught. It appeared to be a female snow bunting. We passed through more ice than we had met with for some time past: it was not, however, in a sufficient quantity to interrupt us, being in loose streams only. Close in with the shore we saw a considerable number of small icebergs.

On the following day we passed a high land, off which, at the distance of five or six miles, lay several islands. The mainland appeared to trend S. W. or S. W. by S. In the afternoon we came to a stream of loose ice, which impeded our progress a little. During the day we likewise passed a considerable number of icebergs.

On Thursday, the 17th, the land was in sight during the whole of the day, but we were at such a distance from it, that little can be said respecting it, unless that it was high, rugged, and covered with snow. The sea was perfectly clear of ice, notwithstanding we were in what is considered the narrowest part of the Straits, in about the latitude of 62°, that is, between Riscoll, on the coast of Greenland, and the south end of what is commonly called James Island. There cannot be any doubt but that the land along which we have been coasting for some days past is what the fishermen call James Island; but whether it is an island or not we have not been able to determine, as we have often lost sight of the land during our passage.

About eleven at night the aurora borealis shone very luminously in the W. N. W. quarter (by compass) extending from the horizon to the zenith. On the 18th we were abreast of a remarkable hill, supposed to be the one called Sanderson's Tower: in one of the views we had of it, it certainly had some resemblance to a tower on a large scale. Its bearings, &c. were as follow.

	o	′	″	
Latitude at noon, by meridian altitude	67	26	47	N.
Longitude, by chronometer..............	61	22′	19	W.
Variation, found at 6·40 in the morning	75			W.

South extreme of the land S. 7° E. (true.) A remarkable square-topped piece of land (query, Sanderson's Tower) near the sea, S. 47° W. (true.)

North extreme of the land, N. 64° W. (true.) Nearest land, S. 35° W. (true) about seventeen miles, making its latitude 67° 16′ 59″ N., longitude 62° 00′ 37″ W.

We passed a flock of rotges sitting on the water, the plumage of which appeared quite different from that of any of these birds we had seen before, they being white about the head and neck, whereas those parts of the others were black.

The wind being light, we made very little progress on the following day, the 19th. The land was seen until half past six in the evening, its southernmost extreme, at that time, bearing N. 56° W. At half past five o'clock, P. M. we tried for soundings with a line of three hundred and ten fathoms: no bottom.

On Monday, the 21st, at eleven in the morning, we saw the coast of Greenland, which then bore from S. 14° E. to S. 42° E. (by compass.) With the exception of a few icebergs, the sea was perfectly clear of ice. A short time before we made the land we observed a hawk, and a small land bird, flying about the ship. The former was shot, and found to be of the species Falco buteo (buzzard.) I neglected to mention that the aurora borealis has been seen every night for some time past. It has assumed a variety of forms, appearing in different parts of the heavens, and shining with different degrees of splendour. It has not been found to affect the compasses, although it seems to have some affinity, not yet accounted for, with magnetism; for, whenever it forms arches, they are observed to be at right angles with the magnetic meridian.

On the following day it blew very hard from the southward and westward (by compass.) Not any land was to be seen: the weather, indeed, during the greater part of the day was thick and hazy, with occasional falls of sleet and snow in the afternoon. On Wednesday, the 23d, the weather became more moderate,

and cleared up in the afternoon, so that we could see the western
land, although very distant, it being by estimation about
twenty leagues from us. One of the hills we descried was supposed to be Mount Raleigh. It was somewhat higher than any other
part of the land, and terminated in a sharp conical point. At
the time this land was in sight, six P. M., something like land
was seen bearing south (by compass,) which was most probably
the coast of Greenland ; but we had so indistinct a view of it,
that we could not positively say it was land. There is little
doubt, however, but that, had we been, at the time the weather
cleared up, ten or fifteen miles to the eastward, both the east
land and the west might have been seen at the same time, as
they were by Davis, and by several others since his time.
This afternoon we crossed the Arctic circle, and entered again
into our native zone. The bearings as they were taken in
the evening, were as follow.

At 6 P. M., being in latitude 66° 26′ 12″ N., and in longitude
58° 15′ 32″ W., the variation 65° W., the following bearings
were taken. South extreme of the land W. 60° N=S. 85° W.
(true.) A very remarkable high-peaked hill (query, Mount
Raleigh) W. 64° N.=S. 89° W. (true.) North extreme of the
land, appearing like an island, W. 78° N.=N. 77° W. (true.)
The whole very distant, but distinctly seen. From the mast-
head, at this time, there was a very strong resemblance of land
South=S. 65° E. (true.)

During the two following days nothing particular occurred.
The weather having been for the greater part of the time very
foggy, we were prevented from seeing the land, on a supposition, however, that we were within the requisite distance. On
the 25th, in the afternoon, two boats were sent to an iceberg
for ice, to be dissolved for culinary purposes.

On the following morning, a suit of warm clothes was served
out to each of the ship's company, by order of Capt. Ross.
I have understood that these clothes were supplied by the government gratis. In the afternoon, I shot four rotges, the plumage of which differed essentially from that of any we had killed
before, the head and neck being mottled black and white, but
chiefly of the latter colour. One of them, indeed, had
these parts entirely white, and in the others that colour prevailed
in different degrees.

There has been, it would appear, a difference of opinion between the French and English naturalists respecting the diver-
sity of the colour of these birds, the former supposing those
with the whitish plumage to be the young birds, and the latter
that all these birds change the colour of their plumage on the

approach of winter. What we have seen of them is, I think, much in favour of the latter opinion, it being probable that, had the whitish plumage been peculiar to the young birds, we should have seen some of them last month, when so many thousands of rotges were daily in our view. It also appears to me that it would be preposterous to suppose all those we have seen lately to have been, without any exception, young birds; and still, agreeably to my observations and enquiries, they have not been without a greater or less proportion of white about the head and neck.

On Sunday the 27th, at one o'clock in the afternoon, the weather having cleared up for a short time, we saw land, apparently a Cape, bearing N. 40° W. (by compass.) Our latitude at noon, by Cole's method, was 65° 43′ 32″ N., and our longitude, by chronometer, 61° 27′ 00″ W. The aurora borealis was very refulgent last night, streaming from the zenith in an eastern direction. It generally becomes visible about nine o'clock, and continues to be so at intervals until two in the morning. Attention is constantly paid to the compasses whenever it is seen, but they do not appear to be in any way affected by it.

On the following day the wind being very light, we made but little progress. The land was indistinctly seen now and then bearing from N. by west to N. W. of us: its general appearance was that of islands, but our distance from it was too great to enable us to decide on this point, the nearest land being estimated to be about twenty-four miles from us. It is not, however, improbable, that the whole of the land we have lately passed consists of a chain of islands; such, at least, is what it appeared to be to us.

It was seen again on the 29th and 30th, but still at such a distance that little can be said respecting it, unless, indeed, that it appeared to be very mountainous: the higher parts were chiefly covered with snow, but lower down there seemed to be a great proportion of black land. Off this part of the coast we met with a considerable number of icebergs on the latter day, our latitude at noon being 63° 50′ 37″ N.; longitude 62° 09′ 36″ W.; and allowed variation 61° W. From the size of these bergs, and the depth of the water, it was suspected that the greater part of them were aground. While passing within three hundred yards of one of them in the morning, we sounded in eighty-five fathoms, and it was estimated that we were then seven or eight leagues from the land. The aurora borealis was seen this morning in two opposite points of the horizon: to the eastward it streamed in bright corruscations, from the horizon to the zenith;

and displayed itself to the westward as a luminous stationary light.

It was again remarkably bright on the night of Thursday, the 1st of October, streaming from different parts towards the zenith. At one time it formed an arch from W. by S. to E. by S., the centre of which was about fourteen degrees above the horizon.

Some parts of the land were in sight during the whole of this day, but as usual, at a considerable distance, the nearest being about four or five leagues off: it consisted of a group of four small islands, which, at ten in the morning, bore from W. 43° N. to W. 49° N. (by compass). Our latitude at noon was 62° 53′ 22″ N. and longitude 62° 52′ 02″ W.: variation 60°.

The weather having been foggy, we had not, on the following day, a sight of the land. A strong ripling having been observed on the water in the afternoon, a boat was lowered to try the current, which was found to set S. W. ½ W. (by compass) about S. 8° W. (true) 8 $\frac{1}{10}$ miles in twenty-four hours.

On Saturday the Isabella made the compass signal to steer S. S. E., which is about the course to make Cape Farewell. From this it would appear that our discoveries are about to terminate.

The weather on Sunday the 4th, having been fine and clear at noon, we were enabled to get a meridian altitude of the sun, by which we found our latitude to be 61° 06′ 27″ N.: by account it was 61° 53′ 21″ N.; making a difference, in three days, of forty-seven miles, a proof of the existence of a southerly current in this part of the Straits. In the afternoon we saw a large shoal of finners, about which a great number of fulmars were flying: at this time they were going to the westward.

During several succeeding days not any thing occurred worthy of notice, the weather was occasionally fine, but, generally speaking, the reverse: the worst weather we had had, not only latterly, but since we left England, was nothing, however, when compared with what we experienced on Friday the 9th. The Aurora borealis had been seen in the morning, remarkably bright, and forming an arch from N.W. to S.E. by (compass). Thus, the true meridian was bisected, instead of the magnetic, as has generally been remarked of this phenomenon. At one o'clock it began to blow a fresh gale from N. N. W., which continued to increase until noon, when it blew a heavy gale. About this time, a heavy sea stove the starboard quarter boat; and at one o'clock another sea struck the ship, and did farther damage to the same boat. It was now deemed prudent to furl the topsails, and bring the ship to the wind under storm stay-sails. At 1·20 we lost sight of the Isabella, which appeared, when we had the last view of her, to be scudding in a direction S. by E. (by compass.) About four in the after-noon, another heavy sea struck the starboard quarter boat, and broke the bolt in her stern-post, so that she hung shattered into pieces, by the foremost tackle, which was cut away to clear the ship of the wreck. By nine at night the wind had increased to a perfect hurricane, with a tremendous heavy sea; and from this time, until five o'clock of the following morning, it conti-nued to blow with unabated fury, insomuch that it became ne-cessary for every officer and man in the ship to be on deck* during that period, in order to be ready to act as circumstances might require.

The length and violence of this gale, which continued to blow without intermission for upwards of seventeen hours, exceeded any thing of the kind ever experienced before by the oldest seaman on board. During its height the aurora borealis shone with unusual splendour, varying its colour from a pale yellow, which was its usual appearance with us, to a bright red, and streaming out in vivid forked flashes towards the zenith. Little time, however, was devoted to the contemplation of this beau-tiful phenomenon; for the attention of every person on board was attracted by the fury of the elements, which every moment seemed to threaten our destruction. And, as if it had been intended to render our danger more obvious to our senses, the light of the moon, aided by that of the aurora, exhibited at times, in a faint manner, this awful scene, of which any description of mine is quite inadequate to convey the most distant idea. The surface of the sea was entirely covered with white foam, and the spray which arose from it completely obscured the horizon, even when the above lights shone with their greatest lustre.

As a proof of the height to which the spray rose, we found, on the following day, the mast completely covered with salt, even as high as the truck; insomuch, that the men who went aloft, when they came down, were like millers, but powdered with salt. The ship rolled so much, that we could not, with any degree of accuracy, ascertain the specific gravity of the sea water at this time; but, from the above circumstance, it would appear to have been greater than we had usually found it.

Soon after day light, on Saturday morning, the 10th, our

---

* In consideration of this an extra allowance of preserved meat was served out to each man, and *the main brace spliced*, that is, a glass of spirits given to each, during the night.

danger appeared equally great, if not more so than ever; for we found several icebergs, and large fragments of ice close to us: fortunately, however, about this time, between five and six o'clock, the violence of the gale began to abate a little, and between eight and nine o'clock, we bore up under close-reefed fore-top-sail, and fore-sail. The damages we sustained from this gale, were, considering its violence, very trifling: the star-board-quarter boat was, as has been already mentioned, carried away. Another whale-boat, which was on the booms, was also stove by a sea; and several small spars and loose stores, lying on the deck, were washed away at different times. On the whole, however, it was impossible to help admiring how well the ship behaved during this long and tremendous storm. At noon, our latitude, by observation, was 58° 42′ N. and longitude 44° 07′ 08″ W. The weather had by this time moderated a little, but it still blew pretty fresh, with a considerably high sea running: still, after what we had recently experienced, any thing bordering on moderation was an agreeable change to us.

During several succeeding days, nothing occurred deserving particular notice. It was, indeed, observed that, since the late gale, the barometer had been unusually low. At midnight, on the 9th, it was as low as 28·95; and for some time since it has been still lower. On the morning of the 13th, at six o'clock, it was 28·65. In the afternoon of the 14th, we passed a large square log of wood: but there was too much sea to lower a boat to pick it up.

On the afternoon of the 21st, up to which time nothing oc-curred to interest us much, a strange sail was observed: on her being first seen, we conjectured that this might be the Isabella; but on our approach, we found her to be a brig standing to the westward.

I have omitted to mention that every night, since we parted company with the Isabella, a rocket has been let off at midnight, with a view to its being seen by her. As she sailed, however, much better than the Alexander, we now thought it probable that she was a considerable distance a head of us.

On the night of the 22nd, the aurora borealis appeared more beautiful than we had as yet seen it. The description given of it in the ship's log is as follows.

" At 9·10 P. M. observed the aurora borealis, a broad arch of which extended from E. by S. to W. by S. the centre being due south by compass, and its altitude 50°. When this had remained stationary for about ten minutes, vivid flashes began to shoot from it, assuming numberless shapes, sometimes in right lines, sometimes like volumes of smoke, and at others

Plate III.

A DIAGRAM.

Exhibiting the third series of Experiments made on board the Alexander, for the purpose of finding the deviation of the Magnetic needle November 2nd 1818 . in Brassa Sound . Shetland . the true Magnetic bearings of the object being 173 .° 16'

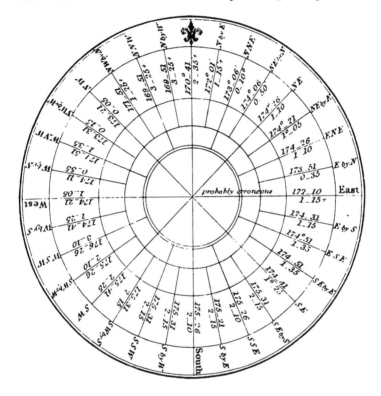

forming segments of large circles in and about the zenith. The colour was generally a greenish yellow, and the light was much more vivid and beautiful than we have ever seen it before.

" The brightest part was at the eastern end of the arch. A stationary light remained about the northern part of the heavens, about 20° high : the compasses were not affected. It lasted, in its most perfect beauty, for fifteen minutes."

On Friday, the 23d, about three in the afternoon, we made the north-westernmost of the Faroe Islands, I believe the island of Vagoe; but the wind being off the land, and the weather hazy, we could not approach sufficiently near to be enabled to say any thing respecting them, unless it be that the land appeared to be very high, and to rise abruptly from the sea.

On the following day we got round the north end of these islands, but we passed them at such a distance, that we did not see more of them than on the preceding evening. They were indistinctly seen on the morning of the 25th, but at a still greater distance.

On Thursday, the 29th, soon after day light in the morning, we made the Shetland islands ; but owing to the distance we had to run, and the wind becoming rather light in the afternoon, we did not get into Brassa Sound until half past two o'clock, P. M. on the following day. In the course of the afternoon, the Isabella came in : she appeared to have suffered a little, as well as our-selves, in the gale of wind in which we parted company, having lost two of her boats.

The officers of both ships were employed, on Monday, the 2d of November, in trying the deviation of the compass. The result of the experiments made by them is exhibited in the diagram, No. 3.

On Saturday, the 7th, soon after day-light, we got under weigh, and by eight o'clock were clear of Shetland.

On the following day, agreeably to the orders issued by Captain Ross, requesting all Journals, &c. kept during the voyage to be delivered up to him, to be forwarded to the Admiralty, I had to close my narrative, which, however it may be in certain respects defective, I may venture to affirm possesses this merit, that whatever I have related as the result of my own observation, is strictly true.

APPENDIX, No. I.

A List of the Officers' Names and Qualities, together with the Number of Men employed, on the two Expeditions to the Arctic Regions.

THE NORTH-WEST, OR BAFFIN'S BAY EXPEDITION.

Isabella.	No.	*Alexander.*	No.
Captain John Ross, ...	1	William Edward Parry, Lieutenant and Commander ..	1
Mr. Wm. Robertson, *(b)* Lieut.	1	Mr. H. P. Hoppner, Lieutenant	1
Mr. John Edwards, Surgeon ..	1	Mr. W. H. Hooper, Purser	1
Mr. C. J. Beverley, Assist. Sur.	1	Mr. Alex. Fisher, Assist. Surg.	1
Mr. Wm. Thom, Purser ..	1	Mr. J. Nias, } Midshipmen	2
Mr. A. M. Skene, } Midshipmen Mr. J. C. Ross,	2	Mr. P. Bisson, }	
Mr. J. Bushnan, Clerk	1	Mr. James Halse, Clerk ..	1
Capt. E Sabine, R. A.	1	Mr. John Allison, Master ..	1
Mr. Benjamin Lewis, Master	1	Mr. Joseph Phillips, Mate ..	1
Mr. Thomas Willcocks, Mate	1	Seamen	23
John Sacheuse, Interpreter	1	A Corporal and Four Marines	5
Seamen	38		
A Serjeant and 5 Private Marines	6	**Total**	**37**
A Serjeant and 1 Private Royal Artillery	2		
Total	**58**		

THE SPITSBERGEN, OR POLAR EXPEDITION.

Dorothea.	No.	*Trent.*	No.
Captain David Buchan ..	1	John Franklin, Lieutenant and Commander	1
Mr. J. A. Morell, Lieutenant	1	Mr. F. W. Beechey, Lieutenant	1
Mr. J. Duke, Surgeon ..	1	Mr. W. Barrett, Purser ..	1
Mr. W. G. Borland, Assist. Surg.	1	Mr. A. Gilfillan, Assist. Surg.	1
Mr. John Jermain, Purser ..	1	Mr. A. Reid, } Midshipmen	2
Mr. W. J. Dealy, } Midshipmen Mr. Chs. Palmer,	2	Mr. G. Back, }	
Mr. C. Wakeham, Clerk ..	1	Mr. Wm. Cotsell, Clerk ..	1
Mr. John Fisher, from the University of Cambridge ..	1	Mr. G. Fife, Master	1
Mr. P. Bruce, Master	1	Mr. G. Kirby, Mate	1
Mr. G. Crawford, Mate ..	1	Seamen	19
Master Buchan, (Son of Capt. Buchan)	1	A Corporal and Four Private Marines	5
Seamen	37		
A Serjeant and Five Private Marines	6	**Total**	**33**
Total	**55**		

APPENDIX, No. 2.

Copy of the Paper committed to the Sea on Monday, May the 4th, 1818.

" His Majesty's Ship Alexander, May 4th, 1818, at one o'clock, P. M. in latitude 60° 45′ 30″ N., and longitude 40° 20″ W. Temperature of the air in the shade 45°; water, at the surface 46°½. Strong wind S. E. by S. some sea."

(Signed)   W. E. PARRY, Commander.

English { " Whosoever finds this paper is requested to forward it to the Secretary of the Admiralty, London, with a note of the time and place at which it was found."

French { " Quiconque trouvera ce papier est prié d'y marquer le tems et lieu ou il l'aura trouvé, et de le faire parvenir au plutot au Secretaire de l'Amirauté Britannique a Londress."

Spanish { " Quienquiera ballera este papel, esta pedido de enviarlo al Secretario del Almirantazgo a Londrés, con una nota del tiempo y del lugar in loss quales se halló el dicho papel."

Danish and Swedish { " Entwer som finder dette papierat, annodes at indsende samme unfortövet til Regjeringen i Kiöbenhaven eller i Stockholm, eller til Secretairen of dat Brittiske Admiravilet i London, med Bemœrking angaaende fiden naar, og stedet huor papieret er fundet."

Dutch { " Een ider die dit papier magt vinden, wordt hiermede verzogt, om et zelve, ten Spoedingste, te willen zenden aan den Heer Minister van de Marine der Nederlanden in's Gavenhage, of wel aan den Secretaris der Britische Admiralitait, te London, en daar by te vogen eene nota, inhoudende de tyd ende plaats alwaar dit papier is gevonden guvorden."

---

* In the printed papers this notice was likewise inserted in the Russian language. This was omitted in the MS. copies, on account of the difficulty of imitating with any degree of precision, the Russian characters.

APPENDIX, No. 3.

Copy of a Letter, or Journal, from Mr. William Baffin, addressed either to Mr. Sanderson, or to Sir John Wolstenholm, they having been, as is understood, co-partners in fitting out the vessel in which he came to this country. [*Greenland.*]

" The first land we saw was in Fretum Davis, on the coast of Greenland, in the latitude of 65° 21'. We prosecuting our voyage were loath to come to anchor as yet, although the wind was contrary, but still plyed to the northward until we came into 70° 20': there we came to anchor in a fair sound, near the place Master Davis called the London Coast. At this place we stayed two days, in which time we took in fresh water and other necessaries : here we had some dislike to the passage, because the tides are so small, as not rising above eight or nine feet, and keep no certain course ; but the nearest time of high water on the change day is at a quarter of an hour past nine, and the flood cometh from the southward. The 22nd day, at a north sun, we set sail, and plyed to the northward, the wind being right against us as we stood off and on. Having not stood past three or four leagues north-westward, we came to the ice ; then we tacked, and stood to the shoreward : a sore storm ensued. By the 30th day in the afternoon we came fair by Hope Sanderson, the farthest land Master Davis was at, lying between 72° and 73°; and that evening, by a north sun, we came to much ice, which we put into, plying all the next day to get through it. The first of June we were clear of the ice before named, and not far from the shore, the wind blowing hard at N. N. E. There we put in among divers islands : the people, seeing us, fled away, leaving behind their tents, and upon a small rock they hid two young maids, or women. This place we called Womens Island : it lyeth in the latitude of 72° 45'. Here the flood cometh from the southward : at neap tides the water riseth but six or seven feet, and S. S. E. moon maketh a full sea."

" Upon the 4th day we set sail from thence, having very fair weather, although the winds were contrary, and plyed to and fro between the ice and the land, being as it were a channel of seven or eight leagues broad. Then on the 9th, being in the latitude of 74° 4' N., and being much pestered with ice, near into the small islands, lying eight miles from the shore, we came to anchor near them. Here the tides were very small, especially the flood, yet the ebb runneth with an indifferent stream : the cause thereof, in my opinion, is the great abundance of snow melting on the land all this part of the year."

" The tenth day we sailed from thence, and stood through much ice to the westward, to try if that, further from the shore, we might proceed : but this attempt was soon quelled, for the more ice we went through, the thicker it was, till we could see no place to put the ship's head in. Seeing that as yet we could not proceed, we determined to stand in for the shore, there to abide some few days, till such time as the ice was more wasted and gone, for we plainly perceived that it consumed very fast. With this resolution we stood in, and came to anchor, off many islands in the latitude of 73° 45'. Here we staid six days, and on the eighteenth day at night, we set sail, having very little wind; and being at sea, made the best way we could to the northward: although the wind had been contrary for the most of this month, but it was strange to see the ice consumed in so little space, for now we might come to the three islands before named, and stand off to the westward almost twenty leagues, without let of ice, until we were more north, [as to 74° 30'.] Then we put among much scattered ice, and plyed to and fro all this month, still in sight of the shore, and many times fast in the ice, yet every day we got something on our way, nothing worthy of note happening, but that at divers times we saw some of the fishes, with long horns, which we call the sea unicorn."

" And here to write of the weather, it would be superfluous, or needless, because it was so variable, few days without snow, and often freezing, insomuch that on midsummer day, our shrouds, ropes, and sails were so frozen that we could scarce handle them: yet the cold is not so extreme, but it may be well endured. The first of July we were come into an open sea, in the latitude of 75° 40', which anew revived our hopes of a passage; and because the wind was contrary, we stood off twenty leagues from the shore before we met with ice: then standing in again, when we were near the land, we let fall out anchor to see what tide went, but in that we found small comfort. Shortly after the wind came to the S. E., and blew very hard, with foul weather, thick and foggy; then we set sail, and ran along the land: this was on the 2nd day at night."

" The next morning we passed a fair cape, or headland, which we called Sir Dudley Digges' Cape. It is in the latitude 76° 35', and hath a small island close adjoining to it. The wind still increasing, we passed by a fair sound, twelve leagues distant from the former cape, having an island in the midst, which maketh two entrances. Under this island we came to ancher, and had not rid past two hours, but our ship drove, although we had two anchors at the ground. Then we were forced to set sail, and stand forth. This sound we called Wolstenholm's sound: it hath many inlets or smaller sounds in it, and it is a fit place for the killing of whales."

" The 4th, at one o'clock in the morning, the storm began again at west and by south, so vehement that it blew away the fore course, and being not able to bear away, we lay adrift till about eight o'clock: then it cleared up a little, and we saw ourselves embayed in a great sound. Then we set sail, and stood over to the south-east side, where in a little cove or bay, we let fall an anchor, which we lost, cable and all; the wind blowing so extremely from the tops of the hills, that we could get no place to anchor in, but were forced to stand to and fro in the sound, the bottom being all frozen over. Towards two o'clock it began to be less wind; then we stood forth. In this sound we saw a great number of whales, therefore we called it Whale Sound, and doubtless if we had been provided for killing them, we might have struck very many. It lyeth in the latitude of 77° 30'."

" All the 5th day it was very fair weather, and we kept along by the land till eight o'clock in the evening, by which time we came to a great

bank of ice, it being backed by the land, which we seeing, determined
to stand back some eight leagues, to an island we called Hackluits' Isle.
It lyeth between two great sounds, the one Whale Sound, the other
Sir Thomas Smith's Sound. This last runneth to the north of 78°; and
is admirable in one respect, because in it is the greatest variation of the
compass of an part of the world known ; for by divers good observa‑
tions I found it to be above five points, or 56°, varied to the westward,
so that a north east and by east is true north, and so on of the rest. All
this sound seemeth good for the killing of whales, it being the greatest
and longest in all this bay. The cause whereof we were minded to stay
to this island, was to see if we could find any finners, or such like on
the shore : and so indeed this night we came to anchor, but with such
foul weather that our boat could not land."

" The next day we were forced to set sail, the sea was grown so high,
and the wind came more outward. Two days we spent and could get
no place to anchor in : then, on the 8th day, it cleared up, and we seeing
a company of islands lye off from the shore twelve or thirteen leagues,
we minded to go to them, and see if there we could get anchor. When
we were something near, the wind took us short, and being loath to
spend more time we took opportunity of the wind, and left the
searching of these islands, which we call Carey's Islands ; all of
which sound and islands the map doth truly describe. So we stood to
the eastward, in an open sea, with a stiff gale of wind, all the next day,
and till the 10th day, at one or two o'clock in the morning, at which
time is fell calm, and very foggy, and we near the land in the entrance
of a fair sound, which we called Alderman Jones's Sound."

" This afternoon being fair and fine, we sent a boat to the shore, the
ship being under sail, and as soon as they were on shore, the wind be‑
gan to blow : then they returned again, declaring that they saw many sea‑
horses by the shore among the ice, and, as far as they were, they saw no
signs of people, nor any good place to anchor in along the shore. Then
having an easy gale of wind at E. N. E., we ran along by the shore,
which now trendeth much south, and beginning to shew like a bay."

" On the 12th we were open of another sound lying in the latitude
of 74° 20', and we called it Sir James Lancaster's Sound. Here our
hopes of a passage began to be less every day of another, for from this
sound to the southward we had a ledge of ice between us and the shore,
and but clear to the seaward. We kept close to the ledge of ice untill
the 14th in the afternoon, by which time we were in the latitude of
71° 16', and plainly perceived the land to the southward of 70° 30'.
Then we having so much ice round about us, were forced to stand more
eastward, supposing it to have been more clear, and to have kept on the
off side of the ice until we had come to 70° : then we stood in again.
But this proved quite contrary to our expectations, for we were forced
to run above three score leagues through very much ice, and many times
so fast that we could get no ways, although we kept our course due east ;
and when we had gotten into the open sea, we kept so near the ice that
many times we had much ado to get clear, yet could not come near the
land until we came to about 68°, where indeed we saw the land, but
could not come to it by eight or nine leagues, for the great abundance

of ice. This was on the 24th of July. Then spent we three days more to see if we could come to anchor, to make trial of the tides ; but the ice led us into the latitude of 65° 40'. Then we left off seeking to the west shore, because we were in the indraft of Cumberland's Isles, and should know no certainty, and hope for a passage there could be none."

APPENDIX, No. 4.

Order issued by Captain Ross relative to objects of Natural History.

" GENERAL ORDERS.

" It is my direction that every specimen of the animal, vegetable, and mineral kingdoms, which may be found or procured by any persons employed in the ships under my command and orders, shall immediately be brought to me, that I may give such directions respecting their disposal as I may think fit: and all officers going on any service to the shore, or ice, or having communication with the natives, are to use their utmost endeavour to collect and procure any thing which may contribute to the advancement of natural knowledge. And of the larger animals and other objects which cannot be removed, sketches and descriptions are to be taken ; and all such reports, descriptions, &c. are to be signed by the officer, and sent to me for his Majesty's service.

" Given under my hand, on board the Isabella at sea, this 17th day of August, 1818.   (Signed)   JOHN ROSS, Captain."

APPENDIX, No. V.

His Majesty's Ship ALEXANDER, *Wednesday, August* 19, 1818.

H.	K.	F.	Courses.	Winds.	No. of Signals	Remarks and Occurrences. A.M.
1	1	4	N.N.E.	East.		Light breezes and fine weather; icebergs and loose pieces of ice in all directions. At 4, moderate breezes and weather; Isabella N. 2½ miles ; a cluster of small islands N.E. 4 or 5 leagues. At 7, 30, tacked. At 8, moderate breezes and fine weather; Isabella E. ⅓, S. ¼ a mile ; a light swell from the northward. At 9, tacked. At noon, moderate breezes and clear weather ; Isabella W. by S. 1 mile ; highest point of an island, in the middle of sound we passed yesterday (query, Wolstenholm's Sound), S. 5° W. 15 leagues. Group of islands, about eight in number, being the north-land in sight, from E. 2° N. to E. 29° 30' S. the nearest distant 3 or 4 leagues. An open sound (query, Whale Sound), E. 30° S. the easternmost of the above islands being just on the middle of the above Sound.
2	2	2				
3	3	3	N. by E.			
4	3	...	North.	E.N.E.		
5	3	...				
6	3	2				
7	3	2				
8	1	4				
	1	6	E.S.E.	N.E.		
9	2	2				
	2	2				
10						
	...	2	N. by W.			
11	3	...	North.			
12	3	2	N. ½ W.	E.N.E.		

Course	Distance.	Latitude	Long.	Variation.	Bearings and Distance.
		76° 29′ 27″.	73° 14′ W.		(See above at noon.)

H.	K.	F.	Courses.	Winds.	No. of Signals	Remarks and Occurrences. P.M.
1	2	6	N. by E. ¼ E.	East.		Moderate and fine weather ; saw land a-head, trending, apparently, N. W.
2	2	2				At 1, 30, answered latitude 76° 29′ N. longitude 7S° 29′ W., and variation 102°
3	1	4				20′ W. from Isabella, made latitude 76° 29′ N. ; longitude 73° 14′ W., and variation 100° W. At S, tacked. At 3, 45, wind shifted ; trimmed sails. At 4, light airs and fine weather ; Isabella S.W. by
4	...	6	S.E. by E.	W.S.W.		W. 1½ mile. A cluster of islands S.E. ⅜ E. 4 or 5 leagues ; tried for soundings with 200 fathoms-line, no bottom. At 5, 30,
5	...	4	E.N.E.			hove-to, to wait for Isabella. At 6, light breezes and fine weather ; Isabella
	...	2	E. ½ N.			W.S.W. 1 mile. At 6, 40, set main-top-
6				S.W.		gallant sail, and starboard fore-top-mast studding-sail. At 7, 15, strong breezes
	Head E. by N. to W.N.W.					and thick foggy weather, the group of
	3	6	E. by S. ½ S.			islands S. by E. ½ E. 9 or 10 miles. At
7	...	4	East.			7, 41, shortened sail, and hauled to the wind on the larboard-tack, in two reefs of the top-sails, and down royal-yards.
8	4	6				At 8, strong breezes and thick foggy weather ; Isabella N.N.E. ¼ a mile. At
9	2	4	N.W. by W.	S.WbyW		10, weather more clear, 3 B 8 from Isabella ; lowered a boat, and sent her on board. Hove-to ; group of islands S. by
10	2	6		3 B. 8.		E. ¼ E. At 10, 45, boat returned, hoisted her up, and bore up in company with
	Hove to.					the Isabella ; set the main-top-gallant
11		6	East.			sail. At midnight, strong breezes and squally weather ; Isabella E. by S. ¼
12	5	...	F. by S. ½ S.	Westerly		mile, westernmost of the group of islands south 5 or 6 leagues.

To this day's Log is annexed the following Note.

For many days previous to Sunday, August 16, (that is, while we could see no land to the westward of the point which we succeeded in rounding on that evening), it was generally believed, that we had already seen the Cape Dudley Digges, and also the Wolstenholm's Sound of Baffin, because the description he gives of these places, agreed tolerably with the lands we took for them in every respect, but the exact latitude. Whenever, therefore, these places are mentioned by name, *previous to the 17th of August*, it must be understood to mean, the parts of the land which we mistook for those so named by Baffin. Of those which we afterwards came to on the 18th and 19th, there can be little doubt, for it is impossible, in so few words, to describe them more accurately than Baffin has done. I have thought it right to enter this note in the Log-book to prevent confusion.

(Signed)   W. E. PARRY,

Lieutenant and Commander.

His Majesty's Ship ALEXANDER, *Thursday, 20th August,* 1818.

H.	K.	F.	Courses.	Winds.	No. of Signals	Remarks and Occurrences. A.M.
1	4	4	E. by S. ½ S.	W.S.W.		Strong breezes and squally weather, At 12, 50, in main-top-gallant sail, and up larboard clue of the main-sail, and
2	3	6	N. by W.			hauled to the wind on the larboard tack. Northernmost point of the land S.E.¼E.
3	1	4	N.W. by W.			Westernmost of the group of islands S. by W. Each of these lands distant
	2	...				from 12 to 15 leagues. Running, occa-
4	2	...	W.N.W.	S.W.		sionally, through streams of ice. 2, 30, more moderate and clear ; set the main-
5	2	...	NW by W½W.			sail. At 2, 50, a thick haze. Bore up to close the Isabella. At 3, 10, hauled
6	1	4	N.W. by W.			to the wind. At 4, moderate breezes and thick weather. Isabella N.N.E. 3 cables' length. At 7, 15, set the jib,
7	1	2				and down fore-topmast stay-sails. At 8, light breezes and thick foggy weather,
8	1	...	N.WbyW½W.	S.W.		Isabella north 3 cables' length. Saw only a few small pieces of ice during the
		4				morning. At 8, 30, bore up. At 8, 40, out first reef of the topsails. Set top-
9						gallant sails. Crossed royal-yards. Set
	1	...	N.E. by E.			the sails and stay-sails. At 10, light variable airs ; trimmed sails occasionally. Tried for soundings with 120 fathoms of
10	...	6	N.E.	S.E.		line, no bottom. Isabella sounded in 245 fathoms, muddy bottom. At noon,
11	...	4	E.N.E.			light airs with thick hazy weather, with clear sky over head. Isabella in com-
12	1	...	N.N.E.	East.		pany.

Course.	Distance.	Latitude.	Long.	Variation.	Bearings and Distance.
N.73° W.	2 Miles.	76°40′52″	74°50′W.		The north-westernmost Island. N. 82° W. 20 miles. (Not seen.) P.M.

H.	K.	F.	Courses.	Winds.	No. of Signals	Remarks and Occurrences.
1	1	2	N.N.E.	E. by S.		Light breezes and misty weather, with a clear sky over head.
2	1	6				At 3, heard a noise similar to that which the water makes against the ice to the eastward. At 4, ditto weather. Isabella N.N.E. 2 cables' length.
3	1	2	N.E. by N.			At 4, 15, more clear, saw land ex- tending from N. ¼ E. to N.E. by E. apparently trending about W.N.W.
4	1	...	N. by E.	East.		At 4, 40, saw one of the group of islands S. by W.
5	1	...	North.		3 B. 8.	At 5, 50, hove to. At 6, light breezes and hazy weather. Isabella S.E. ½ S. 2 cables' length.
6	1	...	N.N.W.	N.E.		At 7, filled and tacked.
7	...	...	Hove to			At 8, light breezes and fine weather. Group of islands S.E. North extreme of west land, E. by N.
8	1	...	E. by N.	N. by E.		south extreme of ditto, N. ¼ W. Land, apparently an island off it, N.N.W.
9	...	4	Up N.W. off West.			Compasses traversed very dull. At 8, 30, tacked ; out first reef of the
10	}					topsails. Hove to, and sounded in 85 fathoms,
11	1	...	W.N.W.	North.		sand and small stones. At 10, filled.
12	...	4				At midnight, calm and fine weather. A cape on the east land, N. by W. 6 or 7 leagues. Land, apparently an island, N.W. by N.

O

APPENDIX, No. VII.

His Majesty's Ship ALEXANDER, *Monday, August* 31*st*, 1818.

H.	K.	F.	Courses.	Winds.	No. of Signals	Remarks and Occurrences. A.M.
1	1	4	N.E. $\frac{1}{4}$ N.	N.N.W.		
2	1	2	...	...		
3	...	6	...	...		
4	1	6	N. by W.	West.		
5	2	...	N. by W.	...		
6	3	...	North.	...		
7	3	2	...	W.S.W.		
8	1	2	N. by W. $\frac{1}{2}$ W.	...		
9	1	...	N. by W.	...		
10	...	6	N. by E.	S.W.		
11	}		Head from N. to W.	Calm.		
12	1	4	N.N.E.	S.E.		

Light breezes and fine weather. The sun rising, and the horizon very clear, ascertained the following bearings. Land on the northern side of the inlet from E. $\frac{1}{4}$ N. to N.N.E. $\frac{3}{4}$ E.; at the southern side, from S.W. by W. $\frac{1}{2}$ W. to N.N.W. $\frac{1}{4}$ W. A strong appearance of land as far as N. by W. $\frac{1}{2}$ W. The land at the points E. $\frac{1}{4}$ N., and N.N.W. $\frac{1}{4}$ W., distinctly seen, though very distant. A small island (or rock) apparently a considerable distance from the northern land, E. by N. $\frac{1}{2}$ N. 9 or 10 miles, trending to the northern land about S.E. $\frac{1}{2}$ E. and N.W. $\frac{1}{2}$ W. of the southern south and north, the whole taken with Alexander's compass. At 7 o'clock, when sights were taken for the chronometers, the land was set to the following bearings, viz. the southern land of the entrance, being high, full of sharp-pointed hills, and much covered with snow, from S. 55° W. to north 66° W., the land trending here about S. $\frac{1}{2}$ W., and N. $\frac{1}{2}$ E.; more distant land beyond it, and appearing to join it as far round as N. 21° W., the northern land of the entrance being high, but not so rugged as the southern land, and not quite so much snow upon it, from N. 44° E. to N. 84° E., both these extremities forming capes, and the land being much higher towards the first of these two bearings. A small wedge like island off the latter, N. 89° E.; the land on this side trending about N. by W., and S. by E., a point of very distant northern land just touching the small island, and appearing to join the land which has been set above at N. 84° E., the distance of the ship off the northern land 7 or 8 leagues, and from the southern ditto, 6 or 7 leagues. At 8, light airs inclinable to calm: Isabella N. by W. 1 mile. At 8, 40, trimmed sails, and set starboard studding sails, calm and hazy weather. At 11, 30, a breeze sprung up from the S.E.; lost sight of the land; tried for soundings with 200 fathoms of line. At 12, moderate and hazy weather, with rain. Isabella N.N.E. 7 or 8 miles.

Course.		Distance.		Latitude.		Long.		Variation.		Bearings and Distance.
										P.M.

H.	K.	F.	Courses.	Winds.	No. of Signals	Remarks and Occurrences.
1	3	4	N.N.E. ⅞ E.	S.E.		Moderate breezes and hazy, with rain. At 1, the weather cleared up for a short time to the northward. Saw the appearance of a high hill N. by W. At 3, the Commodore tacked: in studding sails, and hauled to the wind; weather more clear; saw the land to the southward, and what appeared a bay, the points of which bore S. 83° W., and N. 81° W. To the westward of this the land trends more to the eastward, (by compass) and was seen as far as N. 84° W. At 3, 40, tacked; at 4, hazy with rain, Isabella W. by N. 1 mile. At 6, light airs and hazy, with a heavy swell from the W.S.W. and rain : wore and tried for soundings with 200 fathoms line, no bottom : lost sight of the land bearing from N.W. to S.W. by W., Isabella S.S.W. ¼ W. 1½ mile. At 8, 30, saw the western extreme of the southern-land of the inlet N.N.W. At 10, extremes of the northern land of the inlet from E. to E. by N. ½ N.; of the southern from N.W. to N. by W., horizon dark and hazy, except at these bearings. At midnight, moderate and cloudy weather, Isabella S. ¼ W. 2 cables' length : nearest hills of the southern land of the inlet (the only land in sight) N.W
2	3	6	N.E. by N.			
3	3	4	N.E. ⅞ E.			
	2	...	E. by N.			
4		...	W. ⅛ S.	} South.		
5	}		Head from W.S. W. to N.N.W.			
6	}					
	1	...	West.			
7				N. N.E.		
	1	...	S.W by S.			
8	5	...	...	N.E.byN		
9	5	...	S. W. by S.			
10	2	...				
11	4	...	S.W.			
12	4	...				

APPENDIX, No. VIII.

A brief Sketch of the Quadrupeds, Birds, and Fishes, seen by those employed on the late Expedition to Davis' Straits and Baffin's Bay.

QUADRUPEDS.

Common Name.	Linnæan Name.	Characteristics.	Remarks.
White Bear.	Ursus Maritimus.	Perfectly white ; length from the snout to the tail (of one of those which we killed) seven feet eight inches, and weight 1131 pounds.	We killed two of these animals swimming at the distance of four or five miles from the shore, and we saw several of them on icebergs, and pieces of ice, at a much greater distance from it ; one, indeed, was seen on an iceberg entirely out of the sight of land.

Common Name.	Linnæan Name.	Characteristics.	Remarks.
Arctic Fox.	Canis Vulpus.	About the size of the English fox, and of a dark brownish colour.	Several of them were seen on Hare, or Waygat Island, and on different parts of the West Coast of Greenland.
Hare.	Lepus Variabilis.	Perfectly white, and considerably larger than the English hare.	Several of these animals were seen on Hare, or Waygat Island, in Davis' Straits, and on the West Coast of Baffin's Bay.
Pine Martin.	Martes Abietum.	Length about a foot and a half, skin of a dark yellow colour.	The only one of these animals which we saw was on the West Coast of Baffin's Bay, a little to the southward of the entrance to Sir James Lancaster's Sound.

BIRDS.

Fulmar, or Mallemuke.	Procellaria Glacialis.	Length one foot six inches? extent from the tips of the wings three feet? a strong bill, hooked at the end; the head, neck, and the whole of the under side of the body, white; the back and coverts of the wings ash colour, and in some the entire plumage of that colour.	These birds appear to be very widely scattered over the northern regions, for we first saw them the day after we left Shetland, and there was scarcely a day, until we returned to these islands, on which we did not meet with some of them. They were seen in the greatest numbers in Davis' Straits, about the places where the whale ships were fishing.

Common Name.	Linnæan Name.	Characteristics.	Remarks.
Eider Duck.	Anas Mollissima.	Rather larger than the common duck : the female is of a dusky brown colour; the forehead and cheeks of the male, or drake, are black ; the crown of the head, neck, and back, are white ; the lower part of the body and tail are black.	Flocks of these birds were seen in different parts of Davis' Straits and Baffin's Bay ; but we found the greatest number of them on a group of small islands off the West Coast of Greenland, in lat. 74° N. where they were breeding at the time we passed these islands.
Tern, or Sea Swallow.	Sterna Hirundo.	Length one foot two inches; breadth two feet three inches; bill red, slender, and straight ; crown of the head black ; throat and under part of the body white ; back and coverts of the wings of a hoary grey ; tail forked.	We saw several flocks of these birds sitting on the icebergs as we went up Davis' Straits.
Foolish Guillemot, or Loon.	Columbus Troille.	Length seventeen inches, and extent from the tip of the wings two feet ; bill black, straight, and sharp pointed ; the head, neck, and back part of the wings black ; the whole of the under part of the body white.	We seldom saw any of these birds until we entered Davis' Straits ; but after we made the ice, we found large flocks of them along the edge of it. They are tolerably good eating.
Greenland Dove.	Columbus Grylle.	Bill an inch and a half long, black and slender ; on each wing there is a white spot ; the inner coverts of the wings and the tips of the lesser quill - feathers are also white ; the whole of the rest of the plumage is black.	I do not remember having seen any of these birds until we got amongst the ice ; they were generally seen in pairs, and are very difficult to shoot, diving at the flash of the pan.

Common Name.	Linnæan Name.	Characteristics.	Remarks.
Ember Goose.	Colymbus Immer.	About the size of a common goose; head and back of a dusky colour; the breast, and under part of the body, white.	The only one we saw of these birds was at Shetland.
Rotges, or Little Auk.	Alca Alle.	A little larger than a blackbird; bill short, strong, and thick; the head, neck, and back black; and the whole of the under side of the body white; the feet webbed, and of a greenish colour.	It is incredible the number of these birds we saw in one part of Baffin's Bay; as a proof of the immense flocks of them that we met with, I need only mention, that in the course of five or six hours (one day), we killed, with three muskets, 1263 of them, 93 of which were killed at one discharge. They were excellent eating; we preserved them by skinning them, and then packing them in casks between layers of pounded ice; from the number of them that we thus preserved, we were enabled to give the ship's company a fresh meal of them two or three times a week, for a considerable time. These birds fed on small red shrimps, and it is probable that it was their excrement that discoloured the snow, for it was where they were so plentiful, that we found it of a red colour.

Common Name.	Linnæan Name.	Characteristics.	Remarks.
White Partridge.	Tetræo Lagopus.	Rather larger than the common partridge : the plumage of the male was perfectly white, and that of the female of a rusty brown colour.	The only place where we saw any of these birds, was on Hare, or Waygat Island, Davis' Straits.
Snow Bunting.	Emberiza Nivalis.	Length five inches, breadth eleven inches ; the male is chiefly white, and the plumage of the female of a dusky brown.	We found these birds on all parts of the Coast of Greenland where we landed.
Ivory Gull.	Larus Eburneus.	About the size of the common güll ; the whole of the plumage of a snowy whiteness.	We saw but very few of these birds until we got as far as latitude 76° N.
Burgomaster.	Larus Glaucous.	Length about five feet ten inches ; breadth two feet five inches ; the breast, neck, and the whole of the under part of the body white ; the back of the wings of a fine hoary grey.	We met with some of these birds in all parts of Davis' Straits and Baffin's Bay ; but we found the greatest number of them on a rocky island, in lat. 74° N. where they were breeding.
Kittiwake.	Larus Rissa.	Length fourteen inches ; extent three feet ; head, neck, and tail, white ; back and wings grey ; tips of the wings black.	We met with some of these birds all the way across the Atlantic, as well as beyond the Arctic Circle.
Boatswain, or Arctic Gull.	Larus Parasiticus.	Length 21 inches ; breadth three feet six inches ; the back, wings, and tail, dusky ; neck, and under part of the body, white.	I do not remember having seen any of them until we entered Davis' Straits.

Common Name.	Linnæan Names.	Characteristics.	Remarks.
Sabine Gull.	Larus Sabina.	Length fifteen inches; extent two feet seven inches; head and part of the neck, of a lead colour; the rest of the neck, under part of the body, and tail white; back and coverts of the wings of a pale grey; five outer primaries black tipped with white.	These birds were found only on one small island off the west coast of Greenland, in lat. $75^{0}\frac{1}{2}$ N. It appears that they are a new species of gull; and I understand that the Linnæan Society has resolved to call them the Sabine Gull, in honour of Captain Sabine, of the Royal Artillery, who accompanied the late expedition.

FISHES.

Common Name.	Linnæan Name.	Characteristics.	Remarks.
Common, or Greenland Whale.	Balæna Mysticetus.	It is distinguished from other whales by not having a fin on its back.	The whale which the Isabella's boats and ours killed, was only 46 feet long. I believe their average length is 50 feet.
Fin Whale.	Balæna Physalus.	Is distinguished from the above by having a fin on its back.	The fishermen never disturb this species of whale on account of its having but very little blubber on it.
Seal.	Phoca.	The length of one which we killed, was eight feet, and circumference five feet four inches: it weighed 846lbs.	We saw an immense number of these animals, chiefly among the ice, on which they frequently basked.
Sea Unicorn, or Narwhal.	Monodon Monoceros.	I never saw any of this species of whale except in the water, so that I cannot describe them well: their skin was spotted (black and white), and a horn protruded from the forehead.	These fish must be pretty numerous in Baffin's Bay; for all the natives of that coast whom we saw had spears made of their horns.

DIRECTIONS TO THE BINDER.

The Chart to face the Title-page.

Diagram I. to face p. 39.—Diagram II. p. 48.—Diagram III. p. 89.

www.ingramcontent.com/pod-product-compliance
Ingram Content Group UK Ltd.
Pitfield, Milton Keynes, MK11 3LW, UK
UKHW042151280225
455719UK00001B/262